D1444442

THE
COUNTRY DIARY
BOOK OF
STENCILLING

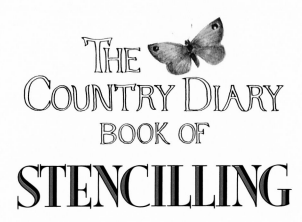

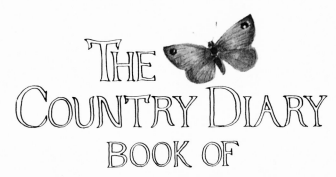

THE
COUNTRY DIARY
BOOK OF
STENCILLING

JANE CHESHIRE ~ ROWENA STOTT

Webb & Bower

MICHAEL JOSEPH

First published in Great Britain 1988 by
Webb & Bower (Publishers) Limited
9 Colleton Crescent, Exeter, Devon EX2 4BY
in association with Michael Joseph Limited
27 Wright's Lane, London W8 5TZ

Designed by Ron Pickless

Production by Nick Facer/Rob Kendrew

The publishers would like to thank Rowena Stott,
Edith Holden's great niece and the owner of the original work
who has made the publication of this book possible.

British Library Cataloguing in Publication Data
Cheshire, Jane
 The country diary book of stencilling.
 1. Stencil work
 I. Title   II. Stott, Rowena
 745.7′3   NK8654
 ISBN 0-86350-179-6

Typeset in Great Britain by P&M Typesetting Ltd, Exeter, Devon

Printed and bound in Hong Kong by
Mandarin Offset

CONTENTS

INTRODUCTION

For most people the idea of stencilling conjures up an image from their childhood. It is a familiar and accessible territory waiting to be rediscovered.

Though stencilling is the simplest printing process in the world it is capable of a whole galaxy of effects from purely naive to distinctly elegant. All that is needed to accomplish it is a little time and patience coupled with the urge to experiment. Stencilling has always flourished in the hands of the individual, it is a grass roots art form *par excellence*. There is no more succinct and efficient way of expressing one's own decorative sensibilities.

In preparing this book we have based our stencils on a direct observation of the natural world. In this if nothing else our work is in keeping with the spirit of Edith Holden's watercolours. All forms of decorative art need to be refreshed by contact with original material. The habit of looking and finding painterly equivalents for what is seen is an endlessly rewarding dialectical process no matter what form its application takes. It only seemed to confirm this tradition to find that American bronze-powder stencillers kept pressed leaves in their stencil kits to be used as outlines for their stencils.

This book aims to present a wide variety of stencilling techniques simply and clearly. All the instructions given are born of practical experience and experimentation with suitable materials.

Every project described is accompanied by one or more stencils. Each stencil is printed to scale in monochrome, so the outline is plainly visible and again in colour for colour matching and shading techniques. Once you have mastered the basic techniques of stencilling and learnt how to measure and mark out the surfaces to be decorated they can be copied, combined or altered to suit your individual projects.

The Country Diary Book of Stencilling will introduce you to the delights of stencilling and of combining stencilling with a variety of paint finishes. We hope it may also be a stepping stone to a new enjoyment of nature in all her manifestations and of the multiplicity of decorative arts that serve to mirror her.

HISTORY

Stencilling is something of an anomaly in the history of art. Like so many good ideas it seems to have arisen universally without any obvious point of origin. Used as a means of printing and decorating it was frequently abandoned in favour of other techniques, remaining perpetually on the threshold of various printing processes. Tracing its history is rather like following the erratic course of a fly, an emerging purpose turns out to be an illusion. And yet it is inevitable, and very much part of its charm, that this should be the case, since stencilling is the most primitive form of printing, and as such, remains within the scope of everyone, artists and laymen alike.

STENCILS IN CHINA AND JAPAN

Before the Chinese developed the production of paper from rags in the second century AD, stencils would have been made from vellum, leather, wood or thin sheets of metal. The earliest physical evidence of stencilling comes from remains in the Cave of One Thousand Buddhas in Tunhuang, China.

Here pounces for applying paint were found

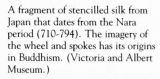

A fragment of stencilled silk from Japan that dates from the Nara period (710-794). The imagery of the wheel and spokes has its origins in Buddhism. (Victoria and Albert Museum.)

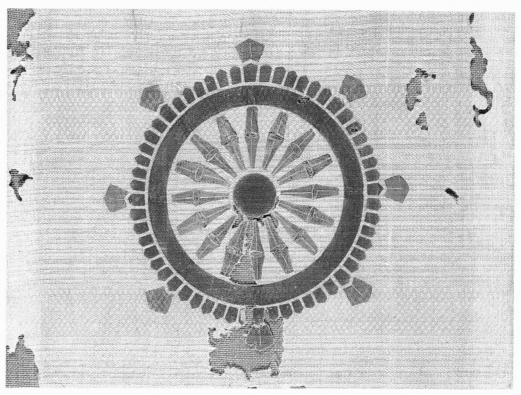

alongside paper stencils. Fragments of silk with the image of the Buddha stencilled onto them were also found and the cave itself contained row upon row of painted Buddhas on its walls, whose essential outlines were derived from a stencil. These date from AD 600 and reflect the emergence of Buddhism as the dominant religion with the establishment of the T'ang dynasty.

From China the spread of Buddhism brought with it a variety of skills, of which stencilling was one. Each country interpreted these according to its own decorative tradition, nowhere to greater effect than in Japan. Here stencilling was rapidly assimilated and reached unparalleled levels of refinement and beauty.

Initially stencils were used to colour leather armour and apply gold and silver leaf to paper. Subsequently their use in printing fabric for clothes in a number of different techniques was extensive and remained unique to Japan throughout the Edo period from 1600 to the Meiji Restoration in 1868. During this time Japan developed in isolation, so techniques that were superseded in other parts of the world by industrial development were extended and refined to an exquisite degree in a country where trade and speed of manufacturing were not paramount issues.

The level of skill and artistry commonly employed in Japanese stencils is universally acknowledged. Traditional patterns were quickly established and remained virtually unchanged over the centuries. Different patterns indicated the season in which the garment should be worn, as well as reflecting the social standing of the wearer. Small designs, stencilled in a rice paste resist on cotton and then dyed with indigo, were deemed to be suitable for labourers and agricultural workers. Pattern and colour increased with social status up to the lavishly decorated armour and clothes of the samurai and their families. The pinnacle of sumptuous effects was achieved in costumes used in the Noh plays, during the peak of their popularity in the sixteenth and seventeenth centuries. For these, stencils were used to gild fabric, and were often used in conjunction with embroidery.

Japanese stencils were made out of paper produced from the bark of the mulberry tree. This kind of paper is still manufactured for katazome, a process of stencil resist dyeing. The paper was made impervious to water by coating it in persimmon juice, which also had the effect of making it more supple. Stencils were cut in stacks of six sheets. After the initial design had been cut, two sheets would be glued together and between them, at quarter-inch intervals, would run single strands of silk or human hair to form a grid supporting the lines and ties of the stencil. After this delicate process of reinforcing, the connecting ties could be cut away, leaving floating sections supported solely by the grid of silk threads, which were invisible when the stencil was printed.

EARLY STENCILS IN EUROPE

The earliest records of stencils in Europe come from contemporary accounts of life in Rome in the first century AD, where writing was taught at school with the aid of stencilled letters cut in wood. Subsequently the emperor Justinian used a wooden stencil with the letters JUST cut in it, in the sixth century AD. The emperor Charlemagne, who was instrumental in bringing about the Carolingian Renaissance of the eighth and ninth centuries, used a stencil of his initials for signing official documents.

Speculation on the uses of stencils in Europe prior to these accounts have never been corroborated. Either much of the decorative paintwork has been lost, as is the case with Greek art, or the stencils were used as a basis for overpainting, so the characteristic ties of a stencilled image are hidden.

It is tempting to claim the negative hand prints left on the walls of caves in the Dordogne, in southern France, by prehistoric men and women, as part of the history of stencilling. Certainly the sense of pleasure and excitement still apparent in them is something that anyone who has stencilled will readily identify with.

The word 'stencil' itself comes from the old French verb *estanceler* meaning to cover with stars or to sparkle and the Latin *scintilla* meaning a spark. A description of the king's chamber at the palace in Guildford in 1256 states that it had 'whitewashed quarried walls, the ceiling painted of a green colour becomingly spangled (extencellar) with gold and silver' and again at Clarendon Palace 'his chamber had a wainscote of a green colour with gold stars (scintillis).' These stars would have been cut out of lead and gilded before being positioned. This elaborate procedure had been abandoned by the fourteenth century in favour

Opposite
Child's kimono from Okinawa, made in the late eighteenth century. The design of water plants and ducks beside a stream was made through a particular method of stencilling known as bingata, or rice paste resist. (Victoria and Albert Museum.)

Top left
Detail from the banqueting hall at Bradley Manor. The room, which has subsequently been partitioned, was originally stencilled throughout in preparation for a family wedding, c 1525. (The stencils with lines across them indicate recent restoration.) The sacred monogram dates from the reign of Edward VI, and is remarkable in interpreting the letters themselves as the body of Christ bleeding from the nails.

of stencilling the shape directly onto the surface with gold size, the varnish used in gilding, followed by the gold leaf. The stencils themselves would probably have been cut in tin.

Recent restoration of the rood screens and ceilings of the Archangel Gabriel's Chapel and St John the Evangelist's Chapel in Exeter Cathedral has uncovered traces of this initial type of decorative stencilling.

The scarcity, and consequent expense, of the materials needed to produce stencils at this time generally ensured they were confined to churches and buildings of importance. The fleur-de-lis stencils in the banqueting room of Bradley Manor, Newton Abbott, are of a later date than the cathedral but are nevertheless typical of decorative imagery from the fourteenth and fifteenth centuries. Of a slightly later date than the banqueting hall at Bradley Manor is the stencilled screen from St Marys Cottage in Newton Poppleford, Devon. Originally this screen formed a division between the hall space and the inner room of a traditional hall house, now divided into cottages. The high quality of its construction together with the stencilled decoration suggest that the house was originally a building of some importance.

Below left
Freehand painting and stencilling used in conjunction in this imitation of a wall-hanging from the banqueting hall at Bradley Manor. It is believed to date from the early sixteenth century.

The screen is stencilled with four repeating patterns, a fleur-de-lis, a crowned M, which is believed to refer to Queen Mary, a five-leafed motif and a flower head. During restoration traces of gold leaf were found, suggesting that the stencils were originally gilded.

STENCILS IN PRINTING

In the rest of Europe, stencils were used in much the same way. But contact with the East through trade, and in the tenth and eleventh centuries through the crusades, brought a steady growth of new skills and ideas.

Paper, previously a rare commodity, became generally available. The first paper mill was built in France in 1200, and the French subsequently became the most prolific paper manufacturers in Europe during the Middle Ages. Contact with the Arab world renewed academic learning as well as introducing board games, dice and playing cards. These new populist activities were largely responsible for the emergence of a new artisan, the briefmaler or dominotier, who has no exact British equivalent. These men and women made playing cards, image prints of religious subjects,

and sheets of purely decorative paper, the precursor of endpapers and wrapping paper. This was the beginning of a popular art. For the first time it was possible for ordinary people to acquire something decorative for their home. A sheet of paper marked out with squares that could be pasted to a piece of wood for board games, or an image print, of a particular saint, who could now be prayed to at home.

Both woodcuts and stencils were used by the dominotiers in their printing. The very first playing cards show the characteristic broken line of the stencil. Stencilling was initially the sole means of printing text and illustrations for books, as well as checked papers for board games. However, printing with wooden blocks rapidly superseded the stencil.

A woodcut had two obvious advantages to the stencil for printing on flat surfaces. It was far more durable, and could be cut to produce a continuous line. These outlines were then either hand coloured or coloured with stencils. There is frequently a wild disregard for colour registration in some of the surviving prints, where the blob of colour, applied through a stencil, lies an inch or more from its outline.

The relegation of stencilling to second place after woodcuts did nothing for its development as an art form. Contemporary workers describe stencilling as tiresome, mechanical and untidy, an opinion voiced later in England by the Painters and Stainers Company.

However, in some hands the stencil flourished. It is rare to come across individual stencillers who were artists in their craft, but, Johan Claudius Renard, a dominotier from Liege, appears to have been one. His speciality was stencilling roses, though his repertoire of imagery was reputedly enormous. Such was his skill that he was granted exemption from tax in acknowledgement for his work and willingness to train others. It was boasted that his work would surpass anything done by hand or by any other means of printing. Sadly, only written testimony of his excellence remains.

Stencils and woodcuts were by no means the only ways of colouring paper; marbling, which had been introduced from Turkey, paste, and embossed paper were also developed at this time, enriching an already prosperous and established trade. In 1586 the dominotiers in France joined with the wood engravers to form a guild of 'Dominotiers, Tapissiers et Imagiers' to protect their mutual interests.

Opposite
Stud and panel screen from St Mary's Cottage, Devon. Originally part of a much larger 'hall' house, the screen dates from the mid-sixteenth century.

Left
The four repeating stencils from the screen at St Mary's Cottage.

Many of the designs and motifs used at this time have their origins in the patterns of the silk brocades imported from China. The influence of eastern design in Europe and the avidity with which it was copied and adapted by European craftsmen continued until the end of the nineteenth century. The stencil, as always, had an important role to play in imitation. It was used in churches, in paintings on rood screens and other wood-panelled areas to suggest rich fabrics on the religious figures depicted, as well as helping to break up any monotony in the background of the work.

Stencils were also used in flocking. This technique developed as a means of reproducing something of the textural richness of the brocade and velvet wall-hangings that were hung as decoration, and draft excluders, in the houses of the gentry. It was based on sound economic principles since it put the selvedges and off-cuts of the woollen industry to good use. Flocking was made by applying size, or glue, with a stencil or woodblock to paper or

Opposite
An embossed endpaper coloured with stencils. This paper dates from the late seventeenth century and is typical of popular German endpapers of the time. (Victoria and Albert Museum.)

Top left
Flock paper from Blithfield Hall, Staffs, dating from the eighteenth century. (Victoria and Albert Museum.)

Below
One of a pair of firescreens made in England in the early nineteenth century. The theorems are stencilled onto velvet. (Victoria and Albert Museum.)

fabric. While the size was still tacky, finely ground up wool was scattered over it. When the glue had dried the excess wool was brushed off to reveal the raised pattern. The same Painters and Stainers Company of London who, in 1600, had decried stencilling as a 'false and deceitful work and destructive of the art of painting, being a great hinderer of ingenuity and cherisher of idleness in the said art' applied for a monopoly for the production of 'flock work' in 1626, for which stencils were required. Though flocking was particularly popular in England and France during the early seventeenth century, it was common throughout Europe. Flocked linen, known as wachstuchtapete, remained popular in Germany and the Netherlands despite the subsequent development of wallpaper. Goethe records its popularity, and even outlined the procedures for its production.

The affluence generated by the expansion of the wool trade encouraged artistic patronage independent of the church. It ensured a cross fertilization of skills as European craftsmen were brought over to work in England, and it is evident stencilling flourished in this context of craft and design with remarkable ease.

Towards the end of the seventeenth century wallpaper came into existence. Initially the small sheets of domino paper twelve by sixteen and a half inches were printed with a repeating pattern and sold in batches of ten or twelve. Later they were pasted together into lengths of eleven and a half yards and sold as rolls. Continuous rolls of paper were not manufactured until the early nineteenth century. Wallpaper was hugely popular and widely used. Savary de Bruslons, a contemporary of Jean Papillon, the man credited with the invention of wallpaper in France, writes in 1723 'there is scarcely a house in Paris, no matter how important, that has not some of it'. This was barely twenty years after its invention. In England too, wallpaper was popular. At the turn of the century the Blew-Paper (sic) Warehouse in Aldermanbury, London, flyposted instructions for hanging wallpaper. These correspond to JM Papillon's watercolours illustrating all the stages of wallpaper production. Both refer to borders at the top and bottom of the wall as well as the sides, perhaps a visual relic of earlier wall-hangings, which

Fragment of a large stencilled wall panel from Holly Trees House, Colchester, c 1800. The design, unusual in that it is executed entirely in stencils, shows the influence of crewel work embroidery patterns. (Victoria and Albert Museum.)

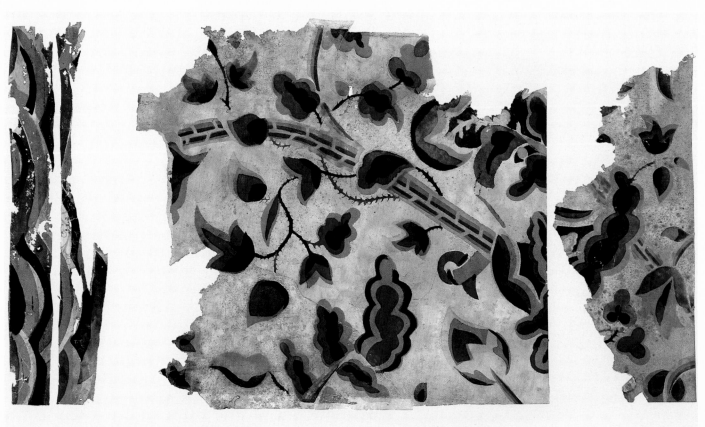

were often bordered. Certainly, at this initial stage, patterns varied from wall to wall. Printed borders were sometimes used independently of wallpaper 'in imitation of a cornish' (sic). Nearly all these early wallpapers were printed with woodblocks and then coloured with stencils, as the earlier decorative papers had been.

From 1700 it was possible to manufacture tinted paper, and many of the flock papers of this time resembled damask in colour as well as design, often consisting of two shades of the same tone. Prior to this only white paper had been available, which was customarily printed with a woodblock to provide a black outline, and stencilled to provide colour. This tradition derived in part from the crewel work patterns that were available for embroidery, and were transferred to fabric by pouncing charcoal dust through a pin-pricked outline. Crewel work was, in its turn, derived from Spanish stitch work. Many of the designs from this period appear to be influenced by the earlier crewel work motifs.

There were other traditions that were also being brought to bear on wall decoration. Blue paint had long been used in country cottages, owing to a commonly held belief that the colour discouraged flies. The Blew-Paper Warehouse took its name from this, and flock papers were often referred to as Blue papers. The rapid development of wallpaper was accompanied by an equally rapid rise in fabric printing and dyeing, particularly silk. Trade embargoes on Indian silks and calicoes bolstered this further and as the idea of co-ordinating wallpaper and fabric became fashionable, the frequent predominance of blue as a colour for interiors continued.

Though wallpaper production and design flourished in England and France, in other parts of Europe its development was slower. This was due to the strong influence of the dominotiers, particularly in Italy, who continued to absorb much of the emerging design skill. In Germany, the Netherlands and Spain wall-hangings of tapestry, leather and flock remained popular. In England, however, wallpaper was such a success it was an obvious source of revenue. From 1726 tax was levied on all wallpaper and continued to be levied, with several increases, until 1862. This defined it as

Fragment of wallpaper from the Old Bell Inn, Herts. Printed with woodblocks and coloured with stencils. (Victoria and Albert Museum.)

a luxury item suitable only for the wealthy. Fortunately stencilling was not confined by this, and from 1700 it is used, not only to print wallpaper but also to repair it where the pattern had faded or been affected by damp, as well as being used by people unable to afford wallpaper as a means of decorating plain distempered walls.

References to the uses of stencilling occur in the many didactic treatises that were published on the general subjects of the decorative arts. Robert Dossie in his *Handmaid to the Arts*, published in 1758, recommends thin leather or oilcloth for stencils. Rufus Porter in his *Handbook of Arts – A Select Collection of Valuable and Curious Arts in Interesting Experiments* goes into more detail and confirms the practice of stencilling floor-cloths:

'To Paint in Figures for Carpets or Borders – Take a Sheet of Pasteboard or Strong Paper, and Paint thereon with a pencil any flower or figure that would be elegant ... then with small gouges and chisels cut out the Figure completely, that it may be represented by the appertures cut through the paper. Lay this pattern on the ground intended to receive the figure, whether a floor or painted cloth, and with a smooth brush paint with a quick vibrative motion over the whole figure. Then take the paper and you will have an entire figure on the Ground.'

Floor-cloths were substitute carpets made out of untreated wool, linen, or cotton, essentially the precursor of linoleum. During the eighteenth century they were manufactured at Braintree, Essex and at Wilton, Wiltshire. They were decorated in a variety of ways, in imitation of marble or parquet, or stencilled to imitate the patterns of woven carpets. The earliest references to floor-cloths date from the early 1700s in England and America.

Stencils were also used on rag carpeting, known as List carpets, which were produced from the selvedge of textile manufacturing. These were usually woven in coloured stripes, with a small stencil occupying the intervening white stripes.

In the *Encyclopaedia of Cottage, Farm, and Villa Architecture*, published in 1836, JC London observes that stencilling is a humble decorative device eminently suitable for decorating cottage walls. Elizabeth Gaskell, in her novel *Mary Barton*, published in 1848, describes John Barton (a Manchester mill worker) as having 'a washy but clean stencilled pattern' on the wall of his living-room.

Several stencilled interiors that date from the beginning of the nineteenth century suggest that it was a far more widespread method of decorating in England than has been generally supposed. Occasionally evidence of original stencils still comes to light under layers of old wallpaper; they are usually executed in distemper onto a distempered wall.

STENCILLING IN AMERICA

The most complete legacy of stencilled interiors comes from New England. Here, during the first quarter of the nineteenth century stencilling was widely and imaginatively used to decorate houses in imitation of wallpaper. Wallpaper was initially imported from Europe, and though it was being manufactured in America as early as 1739, it was as heavily taxed as it was in England. The luxury of wallpaper was outside the income and lifestyle of the early settlers, but the enthusiasm for decoration had a sudden and fruitful flowering in the vogue of stencilling.

Occasionally stencilling was done by the home owners themselves, but the bulk of it was the work of various journeymen of the time who travelled the countryside in search of work. These itinerants were drawn from every level of society, from an individual known as Stimp, who was apprehended for drunkenness and vagrancy when he wasn't stencilling, to Rufus Porter who later edited *Scientific American*. Much of what they did was undertaken simply in return for food and lodging: decorating walls and floors with stencils, as well as repairing furniture or perhaps making small paintings of the interiors they had decorated. Stencilled houses occur throughout New England and as far west as Ohio. Sometimes it is possible to identify the work of a particular individual and through it plot the course of his travels. Certainly the images that were used recur again and again, as designs were shared and copied by other journeymen. Many of the designs used were taken from printed wallpapers of the time, cornices from elegant town houses, classical motifs and conventionalized natural subjects, simplified by the constraints of the stencilling process.

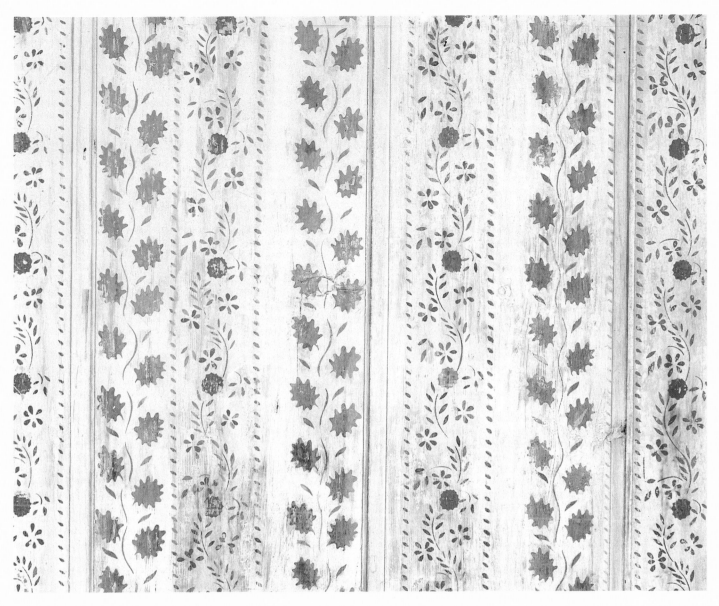

Stencilled feather-edged boards from New England c 1830. (American Museum, Bath.)

The stencilled walls were frequently sub-divided into panels using a repeating border. The panels could then be filled in with separate motifs. Very often a focal point was created over the fireplace by making a large stencil, a vase of flowers or bowl of fruit, and filling it with individual details. Colour was applied in solid blocks without shading. Natural powdered earth clays provided yellow and green, brick dust for red, lamp black for black, while blue was derived from copper and was often fugitive in time. Buttermilk was a common medium for these pigments, the precursor of casein-based paints, creating a flat, sheenless surface that proved to be very durable. Oil paint was reserved for stencilling fabric for blinds, floor-cloths and bedspreads. Among the bedspreads, particularly, are some of the finest examples of American stencilling, with a freshness of colour and design that is entirely their own.

While stencilling on walls and fabric seems to have been done in conjunction, stencilling on furniture was a parallel development, employing different craftsmen. It has its origins in the mid-seventeenth century when Euro-pean cabinet-makers set about trying to repli-cate the lacquered finish on items of furniture imported from China and Japan. The flaw-less surface, characteristic of lacquer work eluded them, though a vast array of recipes involving a variety of glazes and varnishes was assembled to produce a pastiche of the original.

Stencilled bedspread c 1825 from New England. The stencilling has been done in oil paint with additional details added by hand. (American Museum, Bath.)

Stencils were found to be useful in partially mechanizing the process of decoration, but also as a means of applying bronze powder to create a lustrous finish that differed from gilding or freehand application. Subsequently, gilding and inlaying with brass and tortoiseshell became more common in England, but in America the use of powdered metal developed into a distinct decorative art form. Some fine examples exist on hardwood furniture, often deriving the basis for their design from the classical motifs of the empire style, then in vogue in Europe. The popularity of this type of decoration can be gauged by the many factories and workshops that sprung up in the 1820s to supply decorated furniture at an accessible price. One of the best known of these manufacturers was Lambert Hitchcock who began by making chair parts that could be easily transported and assembled at their destination. By 1821 he was manufacturing complete chairs, and employing over one hundred people, including women and children, at his factory at Berkhamstead, Connecticut.

Stencilling with bronze powder required dexterity as well as a certain degree of artistic

An early-nineteenth-century dressing-table from Philadelphia; the drawers are stencilled in bronze powder. (American Museum, Bath.)

sensibility. The best examples create an illusion of depth and form that is not usually associated with stencilling. These were done by master craftsmen whose sets of stencils were jealously guarded to prevent imitation by a rival manufacturer. In time, unfortunately, the need for faster and faster methods of production made this kind of lavish attention to detail redundant. The bronze-powder decoration was applied with a single stencil, and though the images reproduced in stencils became increasingly complex, as the train on the Boston rocker chair shows, the sense of form was never regained by subsequent craftsmen.

The method of using individually stencilled elements to build up a sense of form, rather than simply a flat design, is also used in theorem work, popular in England as well as America. These were done on linen or white velvet, which ages to a delectable peach colour, and were very often framed as pictures. Some care had to be taken with the application of paint to produce controlled shading across the stencils and, as ever with a popular pastime, there were various treatises published offering instruction in the subject.

An American theorem from 1825 stencilled onto velvet. (American Museum, Bath.)

Boston rocker chair c 1850.
(American Museum, Bath.)

By 1835 stencil designs printed on card and ready for cutting were being manufactured in America. They became established as part and parcel of interior decoration. Louis Comfort Tiffany used his own geometric stencils in much of his decorative work, including Mark Twain's house in Connecticut, as well as mass producing designs.

GOTHIC REVIVAL IN ENGLAND

The cessation of the tax levied on paper in 1862 coincided with a revolutionized process for producing wallpaper. Along with the production of continuous rolls of paper, metal cylinders with curved stereotyped plates completely superseded handprinting with wooden blocks and stencils. Production costs were as low as a farthing per yard, which meant that wallpaper was within everyone's means and the market expanded dramatically.

Though production could meet the demand, good-quality design was evidently lacking. There was a preponderance of elaborate prints often exhibiting the florid naturalism beloved of the Victorians. It was evident that manufacturing techniques had far outstripped the

quality of design. Inevitably, as wallpaper became popular it became unfashionable among the wealthy arbiters of taste. Taking its place, very much part of the contemporary Gothic revival, came a return to two-dimensional design, and a re-examination of earlier decorative techniques. The pioneers of this movement in design and architecture were AWN Pugin and Owen Jones, who reinstated the stencil as a decorative tool, elevated now by its historical significance.

In keeping with their medieval associations, stencils were once again deemed suitable decoration for important public buildings, churches, halls, and clubs. The church of St Giles in Cheadle, Staffordshire, has beautifully executed diaper work, done with stencils. William Morris also experimented briefly with stencils in the Hall of Peterhouse in Cambridge.

Pugin and Owen Jones persuaded the wall-paper manufacturers, Jeffrey and Co, to use their designs, many of which were based on medieval stencils and diaper patterns, and established a precedent for commissioning designs from contemporary artists and architects. This was probably a more realistic way of staunching the flood of poor-quality design. The *Grammar of Ornament* compiled by Owen Jones served a similar purpose in providing a standard reference book of design from differing cultures and periods of history. Its aim was to demonstrate how successful design is achieved through stylization rather than observation alone. Inevitably, in redressing the balance, the tendency towards stylization became paramount. Victorian and Edwardian stencils often seem to be a much diluted pastiche of earlier architectural forms.

From a short burst of glory in the hands of the Gothic Revivalists stencils became, once again, the simple tool of many, otherwise untrained, painters and decorators. In *The Ragged Trousered Philanthropists* published in 1914, Owen, the firebrand socialist workman, is a rarity among his peers in knowing how to design and use stencils. *The Modern Painter and Decorator* published in 1930 contains an entire chapter on stencils, along with instructions on marbling, graining and gilding.

Home decorating books of the Thirties and Forties are less detailed in their descriptions of *faux* finishes, marbling and graining, which were, by then, considered too complex for the average home decorator. However, they invariably contain instructions for stencilling, though the suggested designs are frequently bland and unimaginative. By the late 1930s stencils were again being reassessed for their historical importance. In America the stencil work of the previous century began to be recorded and preserved. Sadly, in England the process has been slower, as vernacular interiors and artefacts have only begun to be recorded and valued in recent years.

The process of uncovering the past is perpetual. Invariably, with each new discovery the value placed on the simple satisfaction derived from painting and decorating is re-affirmed. In returning to stencilling as a popular art we are satisfying the profoundly felt urge to decorate, and reclaiming the right to make our individual sensibility manifest through colour and design.

Stencilled wall from the Hall of Peterhouse, Cambridge, late nineteenth century, school of William Morris.

MATERIALS AND HOW TO USE THEM

Right
A range of stencilling equipment including fabric, oil, gouache and spray paint, stencilling crayons, paper, types of stencilling card and a variety of brushes.

Stencilling techniques are easily learnt and with a small amount of patience and practice can be used to decorate a great range of objects and surfaces. A minimum of equipment is needed to begin, and most of this will be used time and again in all of the stencilling projects that you undertake.

The tools required for stencilling have remained virtually unchanged for the last hundred years, except that acetate and plasti-card have by and large taken the place of stencilling card or oaktag, and that fast-drying paint – oil-based japan paints and water-based acrylics – are used in preference to paints that dry more slowly and tend to smudge. However, stencils can be made out of virtually any flat material and printed with any paint, and though the durability of both may not be very great, if inspiration takes you, materials or the lack of them need not be a limit to your ingenuity. As you progress in your skill as a stenciller you will inevitably develop prefer-ences for particular materials and ways of using them. There are no rights or wrongs in this area, and as long as a method produces the results you want it is worth pursuing.

BASIC EQUIPMENT

As stencilling increases in popularity the choices in equipment and paint multiply. You may want to take advantage of the most recent developments, ready-mixed colour shades or wax crayons, or you may feel that these are a constraint on your own inventiveness. Either way, consider all the options open to you before buying equipment.

LAYOUT PAPERS

Graph paper is useful for enlarging designs by hand rather than photocopying and for working

This pretty attic room has been decorated with five co-ordinating stencils. The swags were cut as a single stencil and printed in seven colours using small marine sponges.

out repeating designs. Buy the kind with eight or ten squares to the inch.

Rouge or carbon paper will be needed for transferring designs to opaque stencilling material.

Tracing paper is useful for checking that repeats are accurate and, obviously, for copying designs.

Any lightweight cartridge paper can be used for drawing out designs if it is being done in pencil. If the design is to be painted in order to check the colours needed for stencilling use a heavier weight paper and secure the edges before paint is applied to prevent it from buckling.

Lining paper and/or newsprint will be needed to make rough proofs of the stencil and experiment with different ways of using the design. It will also be needed for protecting the surrounding area while you are stencilling.

MATERIALS FOR DRAWING AND CUTTING STENCILS

Stencilling Card and Oaktag

Stencilling card is the traditional material for stencilling in England. It is made of thick manilla paper soaked in linseed oil and has a beautifully dappled appearance and pleasant smell. Since it holds its shape when cut and doesn't buckle, it is excellent for large wall stencils cut in a single sheet and is generally suitable for simple designs. Because it is opaque, registration marks must be cut for printing. Tracing is necessary for transferring a design to the surface. Oaktag is a heavy paper used for folders and commercial letter stencils. It has the same advantages and disadvantages as stencilling card.

Mylar®

Mylar® is a clear acetate with a frosted matt backing. It is available in a variety of gauges – .004 or .005 are suitable for cutting stencils. Use it with the shiny side up when stencilling. The frosted side can be drawn on in pencil. It is the perfect material for small intricate stencils as it is so easy to cut and is virtually transparent.

Acetate

Acetate, a clear plastic film, is also available in

different gauges or thicknesses. Always buy it in flat sheets rather than rolls, which can be hard to flatten out. Use a .0075 gauge or equivalent medium thickness for most stencils. A thicker gauge can be used for large open stencils, though it will be harder to cut. Avoid using very thin sheets as they tear easily.

Acetate can only be drawn onto with a spirit-based (permanent ink) felt-tipped pen or a rapidograph – pencil or biro simply slide off it. Take care to clean off any ink marks that remain after the stencil has been cut or they will muddy the colours used in stencilling. Some photocopiers can print directly onto acetate, which cuts out the middle process of drawing the design onto the surface. Its transparency is definitely an advantage for registering different stencils and for lining up stencils along guidelines.

Plasticard

Plasticard is a semi-transparent plastic sold in sheets of different gauges, a .010 gauge is suitable for all types of stencilling. It is generally used in model-making and is available in shops stocking model-making equipment. It is transparent enough to trace onto directly, with either pencil or pen. Though not an orthodox stencilling material, it has proved to be ideal, as it is less brittle than acetate and easier to cut than either acetate or stencilling card. (Not widely available in the United States.)

Paper and Card

Paper or thin card is perfectly adequate for a stencil that will only be used once, but in order to extend its life it needs to be made impervious to oil- and water-based paints. The quickest way is to apply a coat of shellac to both sides of the stencil.

Miscellany

Lace or any open-textured surface can be turned into a stencil in the following way: pin the material securely to a frame or board; apply two coats of shellac, allowing each coat to dry between applications; turn the material over and repeat the process on the other side.

Leaves can be used to make negative stencils by pressing them between books or in a flower press for at least two weeks. A coat of shellac or a spray with a cannister of polyurethane varnish will extend their stencilling life.

This detail of purple vetch shows the crisp colour separation created when two stencils are used.

SIZE OF STENCIL
Whatever material is used, always leave a margin of one or two inches around the image to prevent paint going over the edge.

CUTTING SURFACES
Before starting to cut a stencil, ensure the surface at which you are working is adequately protected. It can be as simple as a sheet of thick card or plastic, though both of these will deteriorate in time and eventually interfere with the smooth action of the knife.

A sheet of glass at least three-eights of an inch thick and approximately eight inches by twelve inches provides an ideal surface, though it does blunt the knife. Tape its edges with masking tape, so that they are visible and harmless and place it over a piece of folded cloth while cutting.

A self-healing cutting mat is the best investment, especially if you will be cutting several stencils. These do not deteriorate with any amount of use, and have a grid printed on the surface, useful for checking right angles and registration.

CUTTING A STENCIL
Use disposable craft knives (or X-acto® knife) for cutting the stencils, or a steel scalpel with disposable blades. Make sure the handle is comfortable when the knife is being used with pressure, old-fashioned Stanley knives tend to be much too cumbersome. Choose blades that have a short cutting edge to reduce the chance of them wobbling or snapping while in use. Change blades frequently while you are cutting stencils; a perfectly sharp blade is eighty per cent of the cutting work.

An overall pattern is produced by printing this design of purple vetch along diagonal lines. This kind of stencilling definitely benefits from accurate guidelines, but once these are drawn stencilling is quick and easy.

Cut stencils from the centre of the design to the edges, cutting small areas first. Cut by drawing the knife towards you in a firm even pressure, turning the stencil as you cut.

MATERIALS FOR APPLYING PAINT

Stencils can be printed with brushes, marine sponges or spray cannisters. It is also possible to use rollers, particularly on large floor-stencils.

Brushes

Brushes for stencilling should be made of pure bristle at least one inch in length. They should have a round stock and be flat ended to distribute the colour evenly. The best brushes have the ends split into flags to provide maximum coverage.

If you cannot find brushes that are specifically designed for stencilling it is perfectly possible to adapt a variety of brushes to your purpose. Use either the stubby painting brushes sold in children's toy shops, or cheap multi-purpose brushes sold in paint supply and hardware shops. Cheap shaving brushes, the kind that are obviously not made of badger hair, are ideal for stencilling.

It is essential to have a separate brush for each colour in the stencil and advisable to have a selection of sizes: two inch, one inch and half-inch should cover most stencilling requirements.

Always clean brushes thoroughly at the end of each session, making sure there is no residual pigment left close to the stock where it can creep out to muddy subsequent colours. Keep brushes for oil- and water-based paints separate, that way they are less likely to become stiff and brittle; always reserve at least one brush for the very palest shades only.

Marine Sponges

Marine sponges can be used to apply paint as successfully as brushes. They should be dampened before use and then squeezed dry in a clean cloth to ensure the moisture in them will not dilute the paint and make it too wet.

Both brushes and sponges will need wiping clean from time to time while you are stencilling as dry paint will accumulate on them. Keep a cloth dampened with water or white spirit handy for this purpose. If you need to have a thorough wash up in the middle of stencilling take great care to dry the brush or sponge thoroughly before resuming.

PAINTS

Japan Paints

These are fast-drying oil-based paints, which makes them ideal for stencilling. They are available in a standard colour range but can also be mixed with small amounts of artist's oil paint to produce a wider spectrum of colour. Japan paints are ideal for stencilling woodwork, furniture and floors and dry to a resilient finish.

Signwriter's Paint

Very tough, opaque, fast-drying oil-based paint with a limited colour range. The colours tend to become muddy when they are mixed. Use them for floor stencils or anywhere that will receive extensive wear and tear.

Artist's Oil Paints

This is the best range of colours available in oil paint. These are pure pigments bound in linseed oil. The oil content means they are too slow drying to be used directly for stencilling, though they can be used to tint any other oil-based paint, particularly Japan paint. If Japan paints are not easily available or the colour you want can only be mixed in artist's oils, you can adapt them for stencilling in the following way: squeeze the oil colours required onto a sheet of blotting paper or kitchen towel an hour or so before using them, so that most of the linseed oil is soaked up; then mix the pigment with Japan gold size and a drop of liquid paint drier. This will provide a thick, relatively fast-drying paint, which is more translucent than Japan or acrylic paint.

Stencil Crayons

These are oil-based wax crayons which can be used on most interior surfaces, wood, walls, paper, etc. A small amount of the soft wax is rubbed onto the stencil, but away from the cut areas. It is then picked up by the brush and applied in the usual manner. Its dryness ensures the stencil is printed clearly, making it a virtually foolproof method for beginners.

These crayons are available in a wide colour range and can be overprinted immediately to produce deeper colours and tones. After use the brush should be washed in white spirit and the stencil wiped clean.

All of the above paints are soluble in white spirits (mineral spirits) or turpentine.

These lovely images on glass (by Susie Bower of GlassScapes) were made by a reverse stencilling process in which the image is masked off and the surrounding glass sandblasted.

Acrylic Paints

These are fast-drying water-based paints that will adhere satisfactorily to most painted surfaces. They dry to a waterproof, slightly glossy finish and can be used without varnish on walls. If, however, they are used on floors or furniture they will need several protective coats of varnish.

Their rapid drying time can be extended by the addition of a medium that retards drying. Even then it is still advisable to squeeze out the paint in small quantities at a time to avoid waste. Stop at regular intervals to wash out both the brush and the stencil to prevent dry paint from clogging either. Acrylic paint premixed to subtle, rather chalky colours is available at some stencil supply shops.

Gouache Paints

These are opaque, matt paints in a water-based medium. As with artist's oils they are composed of pure pigment and consequently their colour range and mixing quality are superior to that of acrylic paint. Stencils in gouache must be protected with several layers of varnish.

Mixing the gouache with an acrylic medium or using it with emulsion paint as a base will give a less vulnerable surface than using it on its own. Gouache paint dries several shades lighter than it appears when wet, so it is worth mixing all the colours needed for stencilling at the outset and keeping them in an airtight container.

Watercolours

Watercolours are clear water-based paints that produce a wonderful variety of effects according to the density of their application. They should be applied with a slightly damp sponge and mixed with a clear acrylic medium to provide a little body. The quick-drying transparent properties of watercolours can be used in stencilling to create delicate, luminous colours. Watercolours will go onto any smooth surface, but must be protected with varnish wherever there will be wear and tear.

Aerosol or Car Paints

These are cellulose paints and require acetone, or nail polish remover, as a solvent. They are made in a wide range of colours and finishes. Colours are mixed by overlaying layers of fine spray. The paint dries almost instantly and, with care, lovely finishes can be achieved on any type of surface.

Spray paints add a different dimension to stencilling and require a rather different approach. They should always be used according to the manufacturer's instructions in a well-ventilated environment. Mask off an area one-foot square around the stencil to protect the surrounding area and ensure that the stencil is perfectly flush to the surface or the spray will seep underneath it, making a fuzzy print. Shading or blocking-off areas can be done while spraying using a piece of card.

These paints can be used effectively on ceramic surfaces and glass. Apply the paint in several short bursts of spraying to control the effect.

Fabric Paint

There are a variety of fabric paints available. Use the kind recommended for silk screening rather than the thinner dye type and follow the manufacturer's instructions for making the paint fast.

It is essential to use fabric paint for any fabric that will be washed or dry cleaned and generally fabric paint is only suitable for natural fabrics since the paint is usually made fast by ironing at high temperatures.

Ceramic and Glass Paint

These paints are available in craft shops. Some ceramic paints require firing at a low temperature, usually 600°F, which ceramic suppliers will do on your behalf for a small fee. Otherwise use the type that dries to an impervious finish. These paints are less viscous than ordinary paint and tend to run and smudge easily, so apply them very sparingly – in two separate coats if necessary. Aerosol paint can be used on tiles, and is relatively hard wearing. Artist's oils can also be used to stencil ceramics if they are mixed with exterior varnish.

Bronze Powders

These are powdered metal alloys which are available in a range of colours from pale lemon-gold to red-bronze. They can be mixed with gum arabic to produce a thick gold paint or applied as a powder. They are most effective when used on dark surfaces, natural woods, deep shades of green, red, blue or black and provide, at little cost, a luxurious finish to any piece of work. More specific instructions on their use are given in the relevant chapter.

Any kind of paint used to stencil must be applied sparingly to achieve a crisp edge. The most common mistake when starting is an overloaded paint brush, which will inevitably, and dishearteningly, produce a blurred stencil. Always blot your paint brush on kitchen towel to remove excess paint before applying it to the stencil. To prevent colour seeping under the edges use a pouncing movement to apply the paint. In stencils where a solid area of colour is required a bigger brush can be used with a rolling, circular motion.

POSITIONING STENCILS

Use chalk or charcoal to draw guidelines, depending on the background colour. Guidelines should consist of broken dots rather than a continuous line. Pencil lines can be irremoveable on some surfaces. Plumb lines are used to find a true vertical on a wall. Chalk boxes can be used to mark out guidelines over a large area. A putty rubber or kneaded eraser is useful for removing guidelines after stencilling. Always check guidelines by eye before beginning to stencil: very few rooms have consistent right angles. Construct circles and ellipses on paper or card and use them as templates rather than constructing them on the wall itself.

HOLDING STENCILS IN POSITION

Spray mount adhesive, used in graphic studios, is the easiest way of attaching a stencil securely to the surface. It can be used on a variety of surfaces, including fabric, equally successfully. After use it can be removed from the stencil with a rag dampened with white spirit (mineral spirit). It should not be used for stencilling paper.

Masking tape can also be used to secure a stencil in position as can dressmaking pins. Small stencils printed in one colour can be held in place by hand.

PREPARING BACKGROUNDS

Ensure any surface is smooth before stencilling it. Walls should be washed with a strong all-purpose cleaner or a solution of washing-up liquid to cut any grease. Untreated wood should be sealed and primed, sanding each coat in between applications. Wiping with a dusting brush or tack cloth before painting reduces the dust that otherwise tends to settle into the wet paint. Avoid preparing any surface with a gloss finish, use background paints that will give a flat (matt) or semi-gloss (eggshell or vinyl silk) finish, otherwise the stencil paint will not adhere properly.

Floors should not be stencilled without proper preparation. This means either sanding back to bare wood, or scrubbing it with wire wool and a mild caustic solution to cut through layers of wax polish. Some polishing machines have their own instructions for removing layers of polish which will save on elbow grease. If a waxed floor already has one or two protective coats of varnish on it once the wax has been thoroughly removed it is ready to be stencilled. Newly sanded floors should be sealed with at least one coat of varnish, so that any mistakes are not irrevocably absorbed into the wood.

VARNISHES

Stencils need to be protected by one or more coats of varnish if they are on any surface that will receive some wear and tear. Floors, floorcloths, furniture and woodwork are the most obvious areas. Walls generally do not need it, though it can be a sensible precaution if the stencils are within easy reach of small and sticky fingers.

TYPES OF VARNISH

Oil- and Alkyd-based Varnishes

These are available in finishes ranging from matt to the full gloss of carriage varnish, and are traditionally used in decorative painting. They dry in twelve to twenty-four hours to a hard finish. Ranging in colour from pale yellow to toffee, they all, in common with other oil-based paints, produce a yellow effect which increases with time. This can be overcome by thinning the varnish about ten per cent with white spirits (mineral spirits) and/or tinting it slightly with white eggshell or artist's oil paint.

Oil-based varnishes can lift the colour, particularly reds, in stencils done in oil paint. As a precaution, seal stencils when they are thoroughly dry with a coat or two of aerosol varnish, which is available in gloss and matt finishes. Alternatively, apply a thin coat of clear shellac to provide a protective layer before varnishing with a brush.

Polyurethane Varnishes

These are made of synthetic resins and provide the greatest protection, making them ideal for floors. They are available in three finishes:

matt, semi-gloss and gloss. Gloss is the most durable but produces a finish reminiscent of plastic, which can be offset by applying a final coat of matt varnish over the gloss.

Emulsion Varnishes
Usually used over wallpapers to give them a washable finish, these are made of water soluble acrylic and dry to form an impervious surface. They can be used over acrylic or oil-based stencils that have dried thoroughly. Do not use them over watercolour or gouache stencils, these should be protected with oil-based varnish.

Checklist
Graph paper
Tracing paper
Technical drawing pen, a rapidograph or rotring pen, or a permanent felt-tipped marker, or soft pencil
Ruler, T-square and right angle
Suitable material for the stencil, either acetate, plasticard, stencil card, or similar
Craft knife, X-acto® knife, or scalpel
Cutting mat or equivalent
Masking tape and Sellotape, or Scotch tape
Spray mount adhesive
Saucers or foil bowls
Newspaper and plain paper
Paint
Solvent
Palette knife
Brushes or sponges
Paper towels
Metal tape-measure
Plumb line and chalk box
Tray
Varnish and varnishing brush

Check through the basic equipment list before starting a project and make sure everything is to hand.

Techniques
There are a few guidelines to bear in mind when stencilling. Though you will rapidly develop your own techniques and methods for working, read this through carefully before embarking on your first project.

TRACING DESIGNS
Stencils can be derived from an infinite variety of sources. Ways of interpreting designs and

drawings so that they can be used to make stencils are more fully discussed in the chapter on designing. Once you have decided on a design, trace it out on paper so that the outline is clear. It may need to be enlarged or reduced before it can be used.

Tracing should be done with a soft pencil. Lay the tracing paper flat over the design and secure it with small slivers of masking tape. Trace carefully, keeping exactly to the outline and maintaining a sharp point to your pencil. Inaccuracies made at this point will become much more pronounced by the time the stencil is actually cut. If the design has more than one colour, meaning more than one stencil is going to be cut, it may be worth shading each separate section with a rough form of cross hatching to avoid confusion when you come to draw out the separate stencils.

If the design needs to be enlarged or reduced this is the moment to do it. Position the drawing or tracing where the stencil will go and look at it from a distance to assess how appropriate its scale is.

Borders at ceiling or picture rail height often require some adjusting according to the relative height of the room. A pretty border can be completely lost when placed at a height of ten feet, but a slight increase in scale will enable it to hold its own.

Scaling a design up or down is most easily done by taking it to a copyshop or quick-printing shop where, for a very small charge, it will be copied to the scale you require. Otherwise change the scale by using the time-honoured grid method shown in the illustration.

TRANSFERRING THE DESIGN TO STENCILLING MATERIAL
When the design is the required size it can be traced onto your stencilling material. Place the design onto a drawing-board and hold it in position with masking tape. Cut a piece of stencilling material large enough to cover the design and leave a border of two inches all around the edge of the design. Secure this in place with masking tape. Use a pencil to trace the design onto plasticard or Mylar® (make sure that you have the frosted surface face up for Mylar®). Use a rapidograph pen or a spirit-based (permanent), felt-tipped pen, with a fine point, for drawing onto acetate.

When using an opaque material for making stencils it should be secured to the drawing-board

This stencil design has been colour-keyed to prevent any mistakes arising when it is traced off onto three separate stencils.

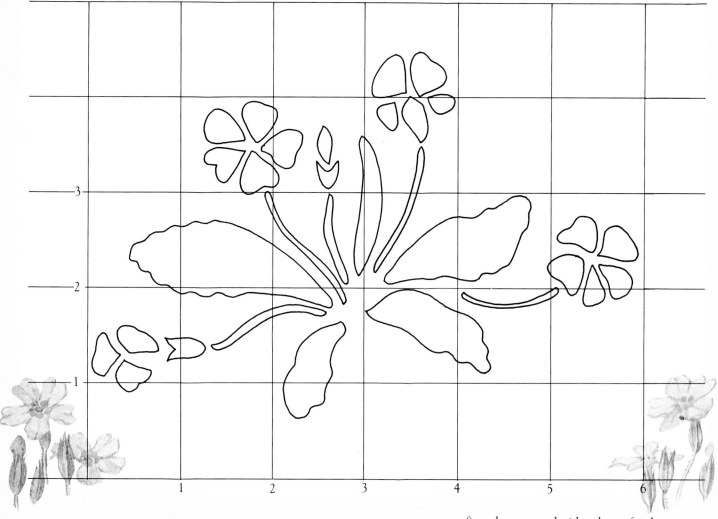

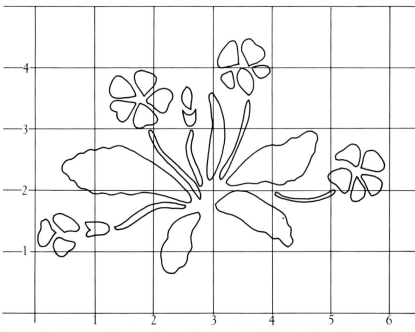

first, then covered with a sheet of carbon or rouge paper that is slightly larger than the design. The inked side must be face down. Secure this and place the design on top, again securing it in position with masking tape. Draw around the outline with a hard pencil or biro. As with any other stencilling material, ensure that there is a border of two inches around the design.

If you are making several colour plates number them in the order in which they will be used. Opaque stencilling material will need registration marks cut in it. These are usually provided by choosing two inconspicuous details from the design. These same two details must be cut accurately in each subsequent colour plate for clear registration, as the illustration shows.

Transparent or semi-transparent stencilling material will generally allow for accurate registration by eye, or registration marks may be drawn on the surface. Notches cut in the top and bottom of the stencil or either side can be used to

line the stencil up with guidelines.

CUTTING STENCILS

Complete all the drawing and tracing processes before starting to cut the stencils. Cutting takes a little practice to master, and it may be worth experimenting by cutting very simple shapes before tackling more fluid, delicate outlines.

Make sure you are working at a comfortable height, and in sufficient light. Equip yourself with a cutting knife that is comfortable to hold while applying sustained pressure.

Place the stencil on the cutting mat or equivalent and hold it with one hand, while cutting with the other. Use the point of the knife to do all the cutting, maintaining a firm, even pressure on it. As you cut turn the stencil, rather than your knife, always working by drawing the knife towards you.

Cut the stencil from the middle of the design out to the edges, that way the overall structure will not be undermined. As the pieces are cut they will either fall out or they may need easing slightly with the tip of the knife. Take care to ensure the corners are cut neatly before attempting this.

Mistakes will, inevitably, occur from time to time. If you have simply gone over a line

Opposite
This is the traditional method of reducing or enlarging an image using a grid system. Number both the grids horizontally and vertically in the same way. Use the numbers like a map reference to check the correct positioning of each line. A photocopier will do the same thing in seconds.

Below
This illustration shows one method of making registration marks for a border stencil. The leaf and berry on the left are actually cut in an opaque stencil or drawn in a transparent one. They should be aligned over the previous print to ensure accurate spacing.

Cutting notches in the stencil itself is a useful way of lining it up with horizontal or vertical guidelines.

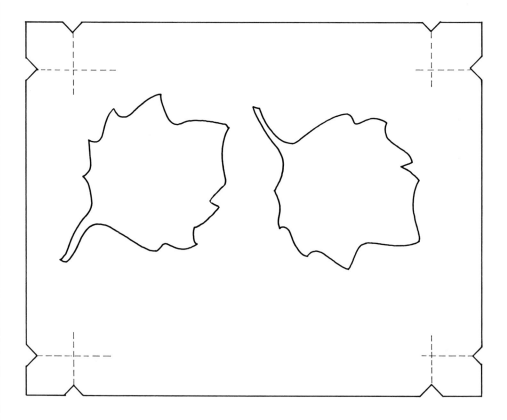

slightly it can be repaired with a small piece of Sellotape (Scotch tape) on each side of the stencil, cutting any excess tape away so that it follows the line of the stencil. If you have cut through a tie, tape may not be strong enough to mend it, and if the tie cannot be cut out altogether it may be worth abandoning that stencil and starting afresh.

At first cutting a stencil seems an exhausting process, and you begin to look on complex designs with a new-found awe. It doesn't last. After you have cut your first ten stencils it simply becomes part of the process.

When the stencil is completely cut, check the underside for any small snags that might remain. These can be removed by rubbing lightly with a fine grade of sandpaper. Carefully clean off any remaining ink or pencil lines.

**MAKING PROOFS AND
EXPERIMENTING WITH LAYOUTS**
Once the stencil is cut out it can be proof printed on paper. This is always an exciting moment, even for old hands. Experiment with

colours and shading, and, if it doesn't have an obvious repeat pattern, with the layout. Often successful patterns can be created by printing the stencil from alternate sides and by placing repeats at half-drop intervals as the illustrations demonstrate.

Tape or pin one or more of these proofs to the surface to be stencilled, and use them to determine the layout of the overall pattern and the necessary guidelines.

There are various ways of organizing the space you are going to stencil. Some people may prefer to place their stencils by eye, others need copious guidelines to work with. Most problems can be resolved by taking a little time, before starting to stencil, to think it all through. The most successful way to work is through combining accuracy of measurement with constant appraisal by eye.

**MEASURING AND MAKING
GUIDELINES**
To make accurate guidelines for your stencils, you will need a ruler, preferably one that is

Unless a stencil has an obvious repeat it is worth experimenting with spacing and layout. Printing from alternative sides will create a sense of movement, while a half-drop repeat tends to be less demanding on the eye.

eighteen inches long, a T-square, a right angle, a plumb line and a chalk line (these last two can sometimes be bought as one piece of equipment). For stencilling small items, a ruler and a right angle are all you need. If the item is small all the repeats can be cut out in one stencil plate. This kind of project is explained in more detail in the relevant section.

BORDERS

On walls, horizontal borders invariably run alongside an existing horizontal: a ceiling, a

When a border is printed round to its starting point it is unlikely to marry up exactly. Either mask off a straight line across the design at the start and finish or fill in the gap to produce a continuous pattern by printing parts of the stencil.

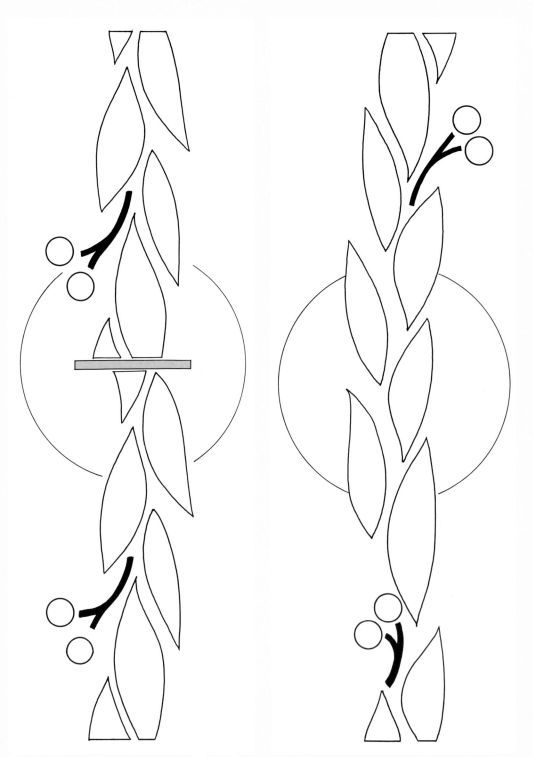

picture rail, a dado rail, or a skirting board. The simplest way to draw a guideline for them is to cut a section of card that is the required width away from this horizontal and use it as a template around the room, lining it up carefully against the edge and making a series of dots to mark the line. Ensure that the stencil has two notches cut in either side to line it up with these marks.

A border pattern that has no discernible repeat can start at any point along the wall and continue round to the starting point. Inevitably there will be a hiatus here, which must be filled either by cutting a small stencil that is a detail of the pattern or by masking off portions of the stencil with masking tape and filling up the gap with individual elements. The illustration shows this in a little more detail.

Where the border has an obvious repeat, such as a swag, more planning is necessary. Usually each wall or side, if it is a piece of furniture, is dealt with as a separate unit. Start by locating the mid-point and space the stencil out from that. Unlike continuous patterns, these designs can take more or less spacing as required to ensure a balanced design.

VERTICAL BORDERS

If these are to go around a door or window frame make a template of cardboard the required distance away from the edge and use it to make a broken line that can be aligned with registration marks on the stencil. If the stencil is to run in vertical lines on the wall, measure and mark the distance between the lines at the top and bottom and then use the chalk box or a

Where the repeating point of the stencil is integral to the design, as in a swag, it should be spaced from the centre rather than one side, to produce a balanced design. Measuring before starting can prevent disheartening surprises.

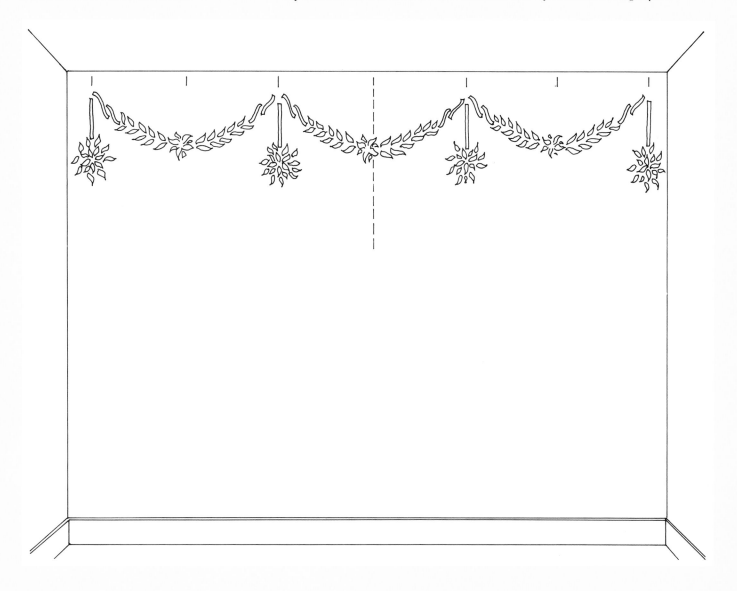

metal tape-measure to make a line between the two points that will align with a registration mark on the stencil. Since the corners of a room are seldom a true vertical, it may be as well to begin measuring from a vertical line made by using a plumb line.

USING A PLUMB LINE AND CHALK BOX

A plumb line is simply a length of string with a small brass weight on one end. The string is held or fastened at the top and the weight allowed to hang. Once all movement has stopped, the string should be held very taut while the vertical is marked.

A chalk box is a plastic or metal container that houses powdered chalk, which can be bought in blue, white or red, and a length of string.

When the string is pulled out it goes through the chalk. This can release a lot of chalk dust, so pull it out away from the area that you are measuring. Only the length of string needed to mark the line should be pulled out. Once this is done it should be held or fastened as tautly as possible between two marked points, flush to the surface. The string is then lifted in the middle and allowed to snap back against the surface producing a clean chalk line.

Use of a plumb-line. The weight should be allowed to hang freely until all movement has stopped. It should then be held taut while the true vertical is marked.

A chalk line must be secured tightly between two points. It can then be snapped, or plucked lightly in the centre to produce a line on the surface.

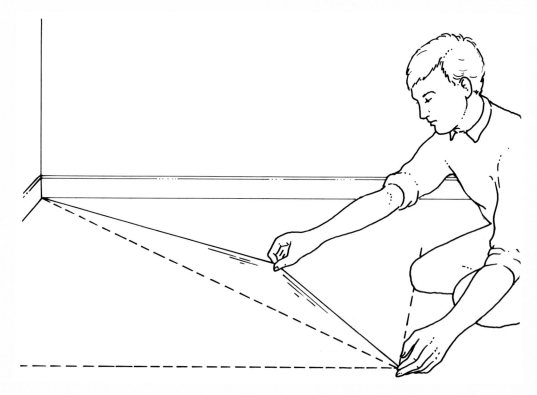

The chalk box can also act as a plumb line, in which case remove slightly more string than the length of the line you want to mark. Secure or hold the string at one end and let the box hang. When all movement has stopped take hold of it firmly and snap the line.

A chalk box is invaluable for speeding up the process of drawing out guidelines, especially on floors. One word of warning, though: chalk can be difficult to remove from certain surfaces, so make a small test first – it should come off easily with a damp cloth. If you are using a chalk box on a very pale surface, mix plenty of white chalk in with the red or blue.

GUIDELINES FOR ALL-OVER PATTERNS

For certain types of design it may be necessary to divide up the surface accurately into a grid that fits the units of your pattern or simply acts as a means of alignment for the stencil.

Begin marking out a grid from the centre point so that incomplete parts of the grid are equally placed round the edges. Failure to do this will produce an imbalance in the way the design is perceived. Locate the centre by running diagonals from corner to corner with string, then locate the mid-point of each side of the surface and join them up. Count out how

many units of the grid are needed, it may be that these central lines will come in the middle of a square. Mark out the grid along all the sides of the surface and join them up, using a right angle to check that the intersections are perpendicular.

A circle can easily be made by attaching or holding a piece of string at the centre point and tying a piece of chalk at the desired length of the radius. Keep the piece of string consistently taut to draw out the circle.

An ellipse is constructed by tying a loop of string around two points, usually pins or nails, and using the loop as a boundary for the piece of chalk which can then describe an ellipse. The closer the two nails or pins, the broader the ellipse. The chalk must be held taut against the string to produce an accurate ellipse. It may be impractical to construct ellipses or circles on the surface itself, in which case make a template on stiff paper or card and use that to mark an outline. Ensure that it lines up with guidelines already drawn on the surface.

STENCILLING

Once you have taken your proofs and marked out guidelines on the surface you plan to decorate, you are ready to begin. If you are using paints that are specifically for stencilling

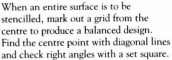

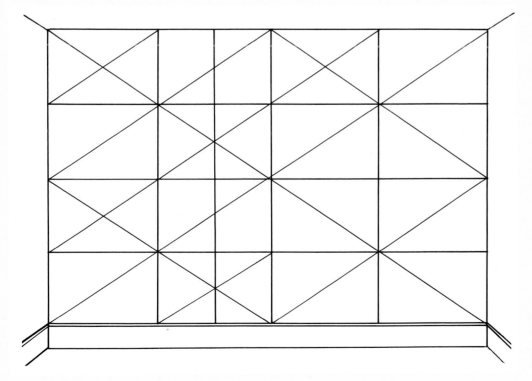

When an entire surface is to be stencilled, mark out a grid from the centre to produce a balanced design. Find the centre point with diagonal lines and check right angles with a set square.

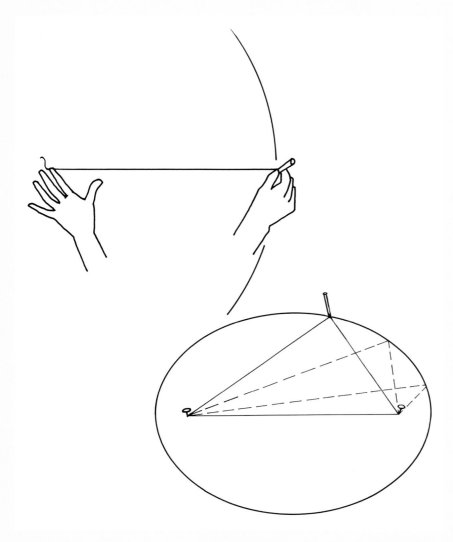

Make a circle by fastening a length of string securely at the midpoint. Attach or hold chalk or pencil at the required distance and keep the line uniformly taut as you draw round.

An ellipse can be made by tieing a loop of string around two fixed points. Hold the chalk against the string and move it round. The tighter the string the narrower the ellipse.

separate brush for each colour, reserving the smallest brush for the most detailed bits of colouring.

Put the brushes and palette or bowls onto a tray along with a wad of paper towels or tissue and a rag dampened with water or turpentine, according to the kind of paint being used. If possible, keep all your equipment for the stencilling project on this tray, so that you know where everything is.

All the colours you need for printing one stencil should be on a piece of equipment that you can hold in one hand. A bucket palette, often used in schools, is ideal, or a plate, as long as the colours are in no danger of running into each other. Separate brushes can be held in the same hand. An overall or apron with pockets in which extra rags, tissues and brushes can be kept is useful.

Dip the brush or sponge in the paint and wipe or stipple any excess onto some dry tissue or rag. If you are using a sponge remember to wet it first to soften it and then squeeze it in tissue to remove all excess moisture.

Successful stencilling is achieved by using minute quantities of paint, evenly distributed on the brush or sponge. The paint needs to be applied in such a way that it will not be pushed underneath the edges of the stencil, thereby smudging the outline. It should be applied with a gentle circular motion, somewhere between stippling and wiping, or a soft pouncing movement, tapping rather than hammering, whichever you prefer.

With practice you will find you can control the quality of your printing completely, so that blending colours across a stencil and shading colours present no problems. To begin however, concentrate simply on producing clean stencils with clear and consistent outlines.

When printing a stencil in more than one colour always work from light shades through to dark. This will prevent pale shades from becoming muddied with dark ones, while dark colours will be relatively unaffected by the small addition of a paler colour.

KEEPING CLEAN WHILE WORKING

During the process of stencilling stop every so often for a clean up. Clean the stencil by placing it on several sheets of newsprint and wipe it gently with a rag or tissue dampened with the appropriate solvent, either water or

they may already be mixed to the colour you require. Otherwise begin by mixing sufficient paint for the job. Don't use a stencilling brush to mix the paint, use an artist's palette knife.

Stencilling is extremely economical on paint but it is worth mixing as much as you will need at the outset of a project, since colours often change on drying and can therefore be hard to match. (Two or three tablespoons of paint should be sufficient for printing a three-inch border around a room ten feet by twelve feet.)

Dilute the paint with its appropriate solvent, either water or turpentine, it should be workable but not too fluid or it will run underneath the stencil and make it smudge. Put a small amount into a bowl or palette and keep the rest covered with cling wrap or in an airtight jar.

If your stencil needs to be printed out in several colours have them all available, with a

turpentine. Do this on one side, then wipe it dry and place it on a fresh sheet of newsprint to clean the other side, also wiping it dry. If you are using a spray-on adhesive for positioning the stencil it may need to be reapplied at this point.

Brushes should never be immersed in a solvent during use, as it will inevitably seep out to dilute the paint once you start stencilling again. Instead, they should be wiped very thoroughly on a rag dampened with solvent. This alone will be sufficient to remove paint that is clogging up the bristles.

Remember to keep your hands clean while stencilling, particularly when you are repositioning the stencil. If a smudge does occur, it can be wiped off, as long as it is small, with a damp rag.

RECTIFYING MISTAKES
Much of the charm of stencilling comes from its identifiably hand-finished quality. Small inaccuracies in registration or a slight unevenness of printing do not constitute serious mistakes and should be left well alone.

Drips of paint can be blotted with dry tissue and then removed with tissue dampened with solvent. Larger areas, (misplaced pieces of the design for instance), should also be treated in the same way. Always blot up as much of the paint as possible before applying the solvent to avoid spreading a huge stain of colour over a large area. Ensure this is thoroughly dry before stencilling over it.

If possible keep a jar of the paint used for the background to touch up any smudged outlines or drips that were overlooked while stencilling.

CLEANING UP
Once your stencilling project is complete always take the time to clean equipment thoroughly before putting it away. Stencils should be placed on several sheets of newsprint and wiped gently with a tissue or rag dampened with the appropriate solvent. Wipe it dry and place on a fresh sheet of newsprint to clean the other side. Even if the stencil has only been printed from one side it will always need to be cleaned on both. Damage to a stencil can often occur through over-vigorous cleaning so work carefully, especially over the ties, where the stencil is most vulnerable.

Spray-on adhesive can be removed with a cloth soaked in white spirit (mineral spirit). If there is any remaining tackiness the stencil can be lightly dusted with talcum powder before being put away. Stencils should be stored flat and interleaved with paper or tissue.

Brushes should be rinsed in water or turpentine, according to the type of paint used. For oil-based paint put an inch of white spirit or turpentine in two or three jars and rinse the brushes consecutively in each. Then blot off all the excess spirit in a rag before washing them thoroughly in warm water and washing-up liquid. Make sure all the paint in the centre of the brush and up around the stock has been removed, if it isn't it will dry hard and make the bristles brittle, thus reducing the flexibility of the brush. Rinse all the brushes well and shake out excess water. They should be left to dry lying flat, away from a direct heat source.

Remove any remaining paint with a palette knife before wiping down palettes or plates. Wire wool can be used to remove paint that has set hard. Unused paint can be stored in an airtight container.

VARNISHING
Varnishing should be done with a brush reserved exclusively for the purpose. An oval varnishing brush, a two-inch household paint brush or a round stocked one-and-a-half-inch brush are all suitable. Oil-based paints should be left for at least twenty-four hours or preferably several days to harden thoroughly, before being varnished. Water-based paints can be varnished as soon as they are dry.

Before varnishing wipe the surface with a tack cloth to remove particles of dust and grit. A tack cloth is a lint free cloth impregnated with a slightly sticky waxy solution that picks up dust. They can be bought already prepared or made by splashing a solution of fifty per cent turpentine and varnish onto a dampened cloth.

Dip the brush about one inch into the varnish and press the bristles against the side to remove the excess rather than drawing the brush over the rim which will create bubbles in the varnish. Apply it generously to the surface, beginning in the middle and working out to the edges to avoid drips and rollovers. Lay it off in a uniform direction, with the grain on wood or vertically on walls. Subsequent layers of varnish may be laid off at right angles to the first to avoid a texture developing. The chapter on paint finishes has a further section on tinted and antique varnishing.

PROJECTS

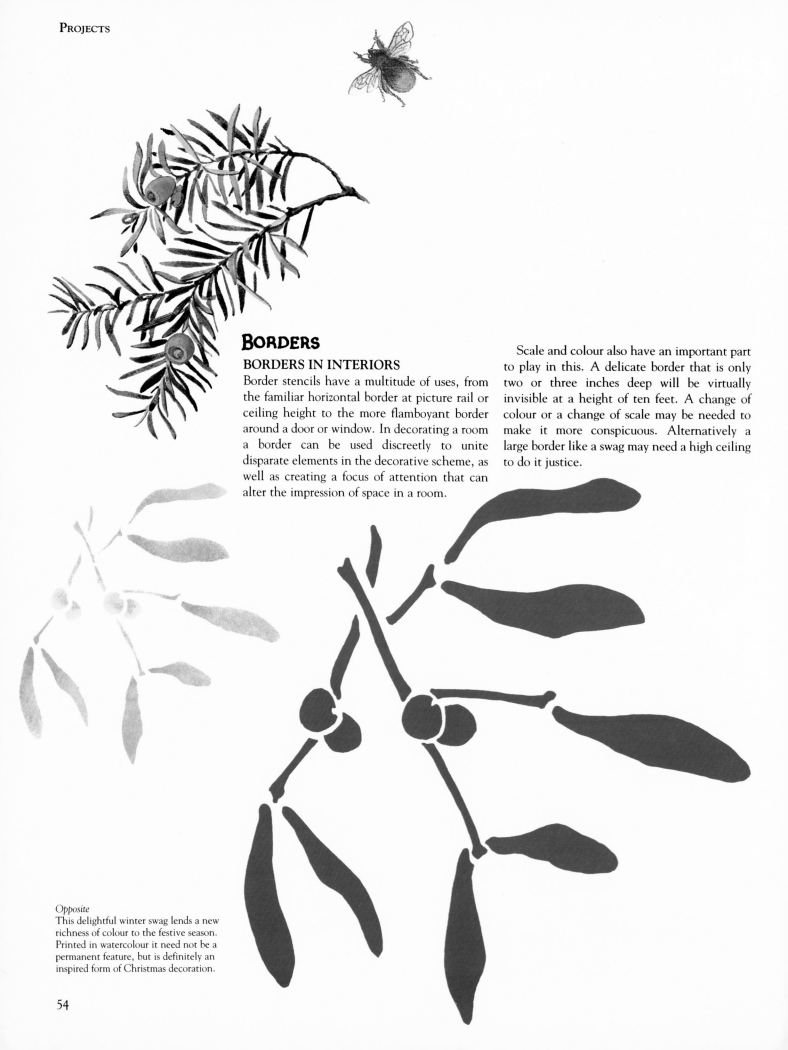

BORDERS

BORDERS IN INTERIORS

Border stencils have a multitude of uses, from the familiar horizontal border at picture rail or ceiling height to the more flamboyant border around a door or window. In decorating a room a border can be used discreetly to unite disparate elements in the decorative scheme, as well as creating a focus of attention that can alter the impression of space in a room.

Scale and colour also have an important part to play in this. A delicate border that is only two or three inches deep will be virtually invisible at a height of ten feet. A change of colour or a change of scale may be needed to make it more conspicuous. Alternatively a large border like a swag may need a high ceiling to do it justice.

Opposite
This delightful winter swag lends a new richness of colour to the festive season. Printed in watercolour it need not be a permanent feature, but is definitely an inspired form of Christmas decoration.

Opposite
This Georgian sitting-room is decorated
with a simple monochrome stencil,
which is nevertheless both elegant and
versatile in this context. It is printed in a
burnt siena wash that is echoed in the
rag-rolling beneath it.

Detail of the willow border. Printed just above the dado rail, the undulating pattern softens the dividing line.

Opposite
An ivy stencil in two colours turns a corner neatly around a fireplace.

Early American settlers used stencil borders in a manner that imitated early wallpaper, though their designs and ingenuity lent them a character that was entirely their own. Borders were used not only at the top and bottom of walls but also to divide the wall space into separate units that could then be stencilled with different patterns or individual elements.

Stencilled borders can also be used to suggest decorative architectural details, types of architraving, cornices and mouldings, especially if they are printed in suitably discreet colours, reminiscent of plaster or marble. These can be placed at ceiling height or used to suggest the borders of panels below a real or painted dado rail.

The great charm of the stencilled border is the ease with which it can be used. There is virtually no disruption caused by printing a border stencil around a room, and no particular surface preparation is necessary. A simple border may take as little as two hours to print out, and can just as easily be painted over and replaced when the decorative scheme changes or your stencilling skill develops.

HORIZONTAL BORDERS

Measure and mark out guidelines for stencilling borders, following the instructions for guidelines in the chapter **Materials and How to Use Them.**

There are two types of borders, those that run continuously and have no obvious repeat point and those that do. The first type should

be started near a corner along the guideline and printed round to the starting point. Very occasionally the two ends will meet up, more often there will be a gap. This can be filled either by masking part of the stencil in a straight line, or by printing a few details from the stencil to fill the gap. If this is not appropriate it may be advisable to cut a separate stencil to fill the gap.

When fitting a stencil around a corner it may be impossible for both ends to lie flush to the wall, particularly if the corner is not a true right angle. Print up to the corner on one side and then reposition the stencil to continue round. The stencil will need to be lightly folded to print up to the corner, but avoid creasing it heavily or it may snap along the fold.

Borders that have an obvious repeat, a swag for instance, are most successfully printed from a centre point along the wall, to ensure the correct number of full repeats are centrally positioned.

TURNING CORNERS

How to negotiate turning a pattern around a corner is largely a matter of personal preference, but there are three options. Simple, chunky designs generally benefit from the straightforward approach of a blocked corner, whilst more elaborate stencils look elegant with a mitred corner or separate corner piece. The illustration on page 61 shows each of these variations.

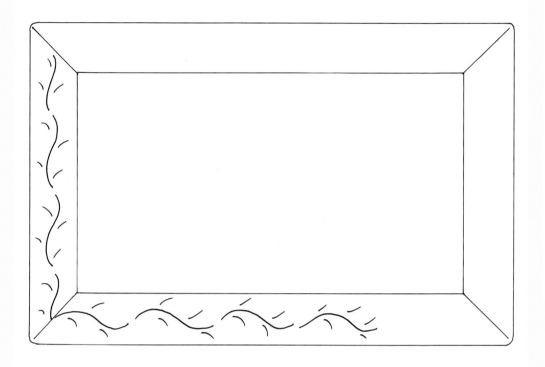

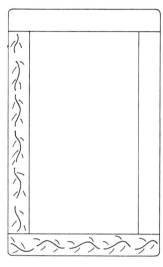

Three methods of stencilling corners. *Above right:* The blocked method is the simplest to do and is most suited to chunky, basic designs. *Left:* Mitring is a more elegant approach. It is done by masking the stencil at an angle of forty-five degrees. *Below:* Using a border design with a specially cut corner piece.

Opposite
A summer swag of dog-roses,
honeysuckle and wild guelder roses.

A detail of the poppy border in strong primary colours that sing out on a white wall.

An elaborate border of pasque-flowers growing sturdily up an archway.

FURNITURE

Furniture can be as successfully stencilled as any other surface with one or two provisos. Choose an item of furniture that has plain flat surfaces uninterrupted by other forms of ornamentation which will detract from the stencilling. Curved surfaces, chair backs and legs as well as some picture frames are awkward to stencil and should be avoided. If the stencil is to be applied to plain, rather than painted, wood ensure the surface is sealed and prepared adequately, and choose colours that are sympathetic to the quality and grain of the wood. (Refer to page 27 for preparing wooden surfaces.)

Use chalk or charcoal to draw guidelines on the surface, in preference to pencil which can be hard to remove. But keep all guidelines to a minimum.

Where possible remove handles, knobs and locks so that they will not be in the way of the stencil. If this is not practical, leave printing the stencil in the awkward areas to the very end and then cut it down to fit snugly around the area, taking care when printing it not to go over the narrow edge.

After the paint is dry remove all trace of guidemarks with a putty rubber or dampened cloth. Stencils on furniture should be protected with varnish. This can be applied over water-based paints as soon as they are dry, but oil-based paints should be left for several days to dry and harden before being varnished.

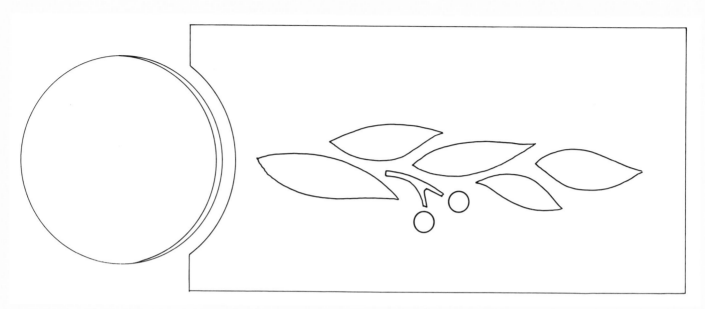

Leave stencilling around awkward areas, like keyholes or handles, to the very end, then crop your stencil down to fit snugly around the obstacle.

Bees stencilled at random on furniture are shaded in two tones to give an illusion of form.

Opposite
This little jewellery box has been painted to look as though it has seen some wear and tear. It was underpainted in deep green and given three further coats of off-white paint before being stencilled and antiqued. Antiquing is discussed at the end of the book.

Stencilled bees alighting on a variety of surfaces.

Opposite
The design of this mirror is based on one which originates from Venice. The frame was painted pastel green, the moldings gilded with gold powder in a gum arabic solution. The green border was stencilled before an antiquing glaze tinted with raw umber and burnt siena was applied and left in the recesses. The result is a convincing fake.

Below and overleaf right
A painted dresser-top stencilled with speedwell flowers and pimpernel border. The dresser has been underpainted in brown, followed by three coats of deep cream eggshell paint. After stencilling, the base coat was removed in parts with wire wool to reveal the base coat. Finally a glaze tinted with raw umber was applied and removed from all but the recessed areas to give a patina of age.

73

Opposite
A border of periwinkle flowers on an otherwise dreary bathroom cupboard brightens it up. It was stencilled in acrylic paints to be splashproof.

Left
Detail of painted dresser-top.

STENCILLING WITH BRONZE POWDERS

This type of stencilling has its origins in the seventeenth century, when the expansion of regular trade between Europe and the East brought Oriental lacquer-ware into fashion. True lacquer is achieved by applying successive coats of tinted resin, prepared from the sap of the lac tree, until a hard lustrous surface is built up. European craftsmen had no access to this technique, but set about imitating it with closely guarded recipes for varnishes and glazes.

Stencilling with bronze powder was used in conjunction with gilding for decorating the imitation lacquer. It was used both as a means of creating a contrast to the lustre of gold leaf and as a way of mechanizing production techniques. It became widespread in America, where it was commonly used to decorate early mass-produced furniture.

SELECTING A PIECE FOR DECORATION
Stencilling in bronze powder requires a smooth and preferably dark surface. For a first attempt choose a small item, a tray, a flat picture frame, or a small box. Simple shapes, without moulding or other structural ornamentation, will present an easy surface for stencilling and will set off the bronze powder, rather than compete with it.

PREPARATION AND COLOUR

The classic lacquer colours are black and a deep red, but deep tones of green, blue and purple can also be effective. White lacquer is not unknown and has recently become a popular collector's item, but on the whole pale buff colours tend to counter the lustre of bronze powder, making it look dull and dirty.

It is possible to stencil in bronze powder over a dark wood finish. To do this remove any traces of wax from the surface with wire wool and methylated spirit. Then wipe it with a damp cloth. Leave it to dry before applying any wood stain, and when this is dry seal the surface with a layer of varnish.

For more complex lacquer effects consult one of the books on paint finishes listed in the back of this book, otherwise prepare your piece in the following way. Cut through any existing layers of old paint, wax, or dirt with wire wool. Check that the surface is perfectly smooth, any irregularities will be emphasized, rather than hidden by this technique. Fill any cracks or dents with filler, sanding them carefully when dry. For a perfect finish apply several coats of ready-mixed gesso to the surface, sanding thoroughly between each application. It is vital to obtain a smooth surface.

If the surface is unprimed apply an undercoat followed by at least two applications of the base coat. Sand well between each application. Then tint a matt or semi-gloss varnish with artist's oil paint or Japan paint to a shade that is similar, but not necessarily identical to the base coat.

Apply this with a soft varnishing brush. Tinted varnish has a tendency to form streaks from the direction of the brush marks. Some early imitations of lacquer incorporate this tendency in the final finish. If, however, you want to avoid it, brush the varnish out in one direction, usually with the grain, then, without reloading the brush, brush the varnish across the grain. Finally lay it off in the direction of the grain. Following this procedure gives an even thin cover as well as preventing gaps in the varnish.

One application of tinted varnish will greatly enhance the colour and depth of the paint beneath. Two applications will increase this still further and are sufficient for the purposes of stencilling in bronze powder. When the final coat of tinted varnish is dry sand it very lightly with a 0000 grade of wire wool.

APPLYING BRONZE POWDER

Since the entire surface will be covered with gold size, it is not possible to mark out guidelines for this type of stencilling. If you will be using several stencils to build up an image it is worth planning your design on paper first and having this beside you when working. Marks for centring can be made in chalk just outside the area that will be coated in gold size, but the rest must be done by eye.

Mix up a solution of sixty per cent artist's gold size and forty per cent turpentine and apply a very thin coat to the area to be stencilled. Size one surface at a time to begin with, always working on a horizontal surface. After some time, usually between thirty minutes and one hour, depending on the warmth and humidity of the room, the gold size will begin to dry, losing its sheen as it does so. Wait until the entire area that has been sized has this matt appearance, then test it on an inconspicuous area by putting the very tip of your finger against it. The size should not be so wet that it leaves a mark, but there should be a faint but perceptible pull when it is removed.

Position the stencil on the surface, the tack of the surface will hold it in position. Have the different colour bronze powders ready on a plate or palette at the same height as your work. Apply each bronze powder with a separate piece of felt, velvet or chamois. This can be wrapped around your finger or folded into a small bob.

Using the bob, pick up a tiny amount of powder and dab it on some paper to remove any excess. Apply it to the stencil in a gentle circular motion. It is not necessary to fill in the entire area of the stencil with powder. The most delicate effects are achieved by simply applying powder to the edges, or to one part of the stencil if it is going to overlap another stencil.

Before lifting the stencil, ensure that any loose powder around the edges is removed. If this precaution is not taken loose powder will fly off and blur the sharp outline beneath when the stencil is lifted up. Work steadily to complete the stencilling while the size is still tacky. It should remain workable for at least one hour.

Once the stencilling is complete it should be left for twenty-four hours for the size to dry completely. Then take a damp, lint-free cloth and wipe the surface very gently to remove any

particles of powder that have not adhered to the surface. Leave this to dry before applying at least two coats of protective varnish. An initial coat of spray-on varnish will prevent the varnishing brush from lifting any further particles of bronze powder.

CORRECTING MISTAKES

Small mistakes, like a slightly blurred edge or a misplaced dab of bronze powder can be dealt with once the gold size is completely dry. Use a damp cloth to wipe persistently at the fragments until they lift; a small amount of liquid scourer can help.

Mistakes that cannot be covered up or easily rubbed off when the size is dry will have to be dealt with there and then. Remove the size and any bronze powder from the surface with a rag dampened with turpentine. Wait until this is completely dry before reapplying the gold size.

ALTERNATIVE METHOD

A tinted varnish can be stencilled onto the surface in the normal way and left to dry until it assumes the matt appearance described above. Then some bronze powder can be picked up on a soft mop brush and whisked lightly over the stencilled size. The size must be sufficiently dry not to move during this process and the brush should hardly come into contact with the surface. When the area has been covered with powder a piece of paper can be placed over the surface and rubbed lightly from the back, to ensure the powder adheres well to the size. Leave the surface to dry for twenty-four hours before carefully removing the excess powder with a damp piece of cotton wool. Varnish in the usual way to protect the surface.

Equipment for stencilling in bronze powder. Three different shades of gold, gold size and bobs. The felt bobs are made by folding a square of felt over a small ball of cotton and tieing it tight with waxed cotton thread.

FABRICS

Stencils have always been used to decorate fabrics. The very earliest surviving stencil fragments are on silk and date from the sixth century. During the sixteenth century in Europe, particularly in Germany and Holland, it was often used as a means of applying flock to fabric for wall-hangings, made in imitation of tapestries. Subsequently stencils were used to decorate floor-cloths as well as canvas blinds; often they appear in conjunction with freehand painting.

Stencilled fabrics dating from the early nineteenth century in America show a high degree of dexterity and skill in their execution. The beauty of many of the designs for bedcovers and table-cloths and the care taken in making them provides a continuing source of inspiration. These early stencilled fabrics were executed in oil-based paints, and, to increase their flexibility, floor-cloths and blinds were copiously varnished and sometimes waxed.

Today there are a variety of fabric paints that are suitable for stencilling and will withstand regular washing. Some, but not all, will withstand dry cleaning. Always follow the manufacturer's advice when using them, and buy enough material to have a surplus for testing colours and techniques. Fabric paints should never be mixed with other paints.

CHOICE OF FABRIC

Most fabric paints need to be ironed at a high temperature to make the colour fast, and for this reason, it is important to use natural materials. Different weights of calico, cotton duck and pure silk provide delightful surfaces on which to stencil. The natural flecks in the fibre and slight irregularities in the weave produce a pleasant background to the stencils.

Natural fabrics are generally sold with starch or size in them to provide extra body. If this is left in the fabric it will prevent the paint from penetrating and remaining fast in the fabric. It can be removed with a hot wash, which will also allow any shrinking to take place.

Colour fabric can be successfully stencilled. It may be necessary to use extra amounts of white fabric paint to give the colours in the stencil enough opacity.

Jersey and other stretch fabrics can also be stencilled. Take care to pin the fabric out so that it is flat but not stretched while it is being stencilled. Obviously when the fabric is stretched out, the stencilled image will be distorted.

Very fine fabrics like voile, muslin or silk georgette can be stencilled. Use a very dry brush to stencil fine fabrics, too much paint will clog the weave. Take care to lift the material away from the printing surface before the paint dries to prevent it from sticking.

Spray paints can be used with success on these types of fabric though they will produce a slight hardening of the surface making them unsuitable for certain projects.

FABRICS TO STENCIL

There are virtually as many opportunities for using stencils on fabrics as there are in interiors; deciding on a project depends primarily on your stamina and secondly on your working area. Small pieces of fabric, such as a table-cloth or a set of napkins can easily be stencilled on a kitchen table or desk top. Curtains and double bedspreads pose more of a problem, since the fabric has to be moved across the table as it is stencilled. For working on large areas ensure there is sufficient space around the printing table, and that the table is at the correct height, since you will need to be standing while you work.

Fabrics for clothes should be stencilled after the fabric has been cut out, to avoid wasted printing and to allow the design to match. Fabric that has already been made up into a garment is not suitable for stencilling, unless the stencil will be confined to a small area, a detail on a pocket or a collar for instance.

Bedspreads, pillow cases, and duvet covers are fun to stencil. It is not necessary to stencil the entire area of each one, a border with a few motifs for the centre should provide plenty of elements that can be co-ordinated. Pillow cases or duvet covers that are already made up should have card or newsprint inside the cover to protect the underlying surface. Similarly a T-shirt or similar garment made of stretchy material should have a piece of card inside it while stencilling to maintain the shape of the garment, as well as protecting the underlying fabric.

HOW TO STENCIL FABRIC

After the fabric has been washed it should be ironed. Then lay it flat on a clean surface and mark out any guidelines that may be necessary

in dressmaker's, or tailoring, chalk. Make a bed of several thicknesses of newspaper or an old blanket folded double on the working surface. Secure these firmly in place with masking tape. Place the fabric on top of this and secure it with masking tape or dressmaker's pins. Any fabric that does not fit on the surface should be rolled up and taped with masking tape and should be directly in front of the working surface. Always work by moving the stencilled fabric away from you.

The stencil can be held in place with masking tape, pins or spray-mount adhesive. As with any other type of stencilling a minute amount of paint is required to produce a clear definition of the design. Effects of shading and modelling are as easily achieved on fabric as they are on any other surface. Fabric paint will dry quickly so subsequent stencils can be printed almost immediately.

When the entire piece of fabric on the printing surface has been stencilled, unroll the subsequent length of fabric and secure it with masking tape. Do not roll the piece you have just stencilled in case the paint smudges.

Let the fabric dry thoroughly before ironing it to make it fast. Very large lengths of stencilled fabric can be made fast in a tumble drier at a hot setting.

MISTAKES
When stencilling fabric, the only way to deal with mistakes is to let them be. Trying to wash out blobs of misapplied colour will invariably spread the mistake over a larger area.

The most common mistakes on fabric are caused by smudges from dirty hands and paint on the underside of the stencil. Don't wait for this to happen before having a clean up, make regular stops while you are working.

STENCILLING FABRIC WITH SPRAY PAINT
Aerosol cans of paint should be held vertically to release the paint evenly. If possible, pin or tape the fabric to a sheet of hardboard or chipboard that can be leant against a wall. Remember to protect the area around the stencil with paper taped to its edges to contain the spray, there should be a border of twelve inches at least. Wear a protective mask over your nose and mouth while working to avoid inhaling the fumes and work in a well-ventilated environment.

Stencil large areas of fabric by keeping the clean, unprinted fabric rolled up in front of you and moving the stencilled sections away to dry thoroughly before folding.

Opposite
A bluebell border and butterflies printed on white glazed chintz.

Five stencils of spring flowers are used to decorate this table-cloth and napkin set.

This tablecloth and the napkins that co-ordinate with it were printed in a half drop repeat pattern using the violet, primrose, cowslip and wood anemone plus part of the pimpernel border.

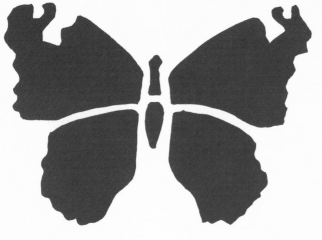

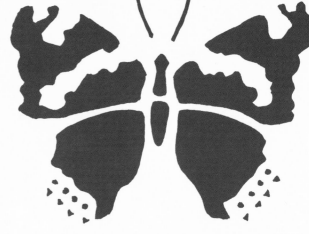

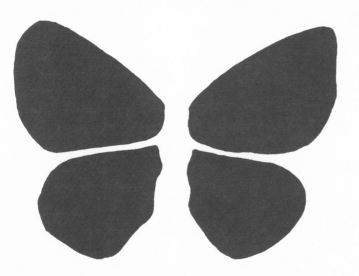

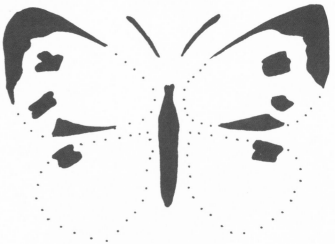

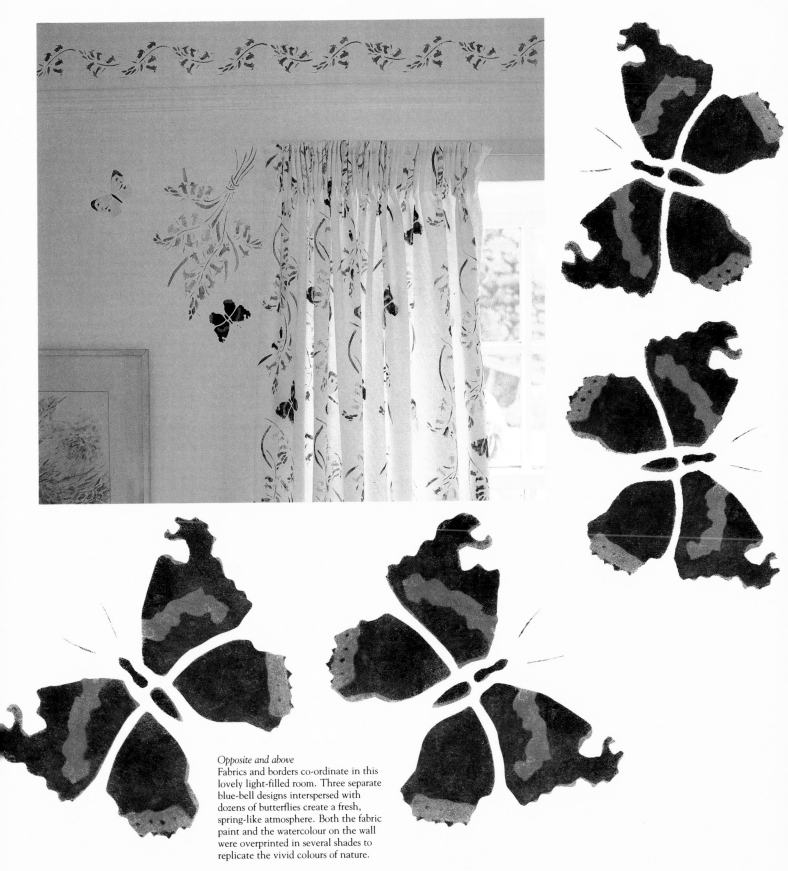

Opposite and above
Fabrics and borders co-ordinate in this
lovely light-filled room. Three separate
blue-bell designs interspersed with
dozens of butterflies create a fresh,
spring-like atmosphere. Both the fabric
paint and the watercolour on the wall
were overprinted in several shades to
replicate the vivid colours of nature.

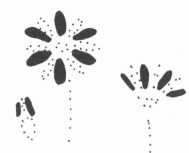

Opposite
Well-dressed bunny in a habotai silk
frock sponged and printed with daisies
that are also used as a bedroom border.

Opposite above
Three stencils are used to produce this theorem in which the usual tell-tale ties of stencilling have been hidden. Accurate registration in drawing and cutting is vital here. Small details, the stamens on the flowers and veins on the leaves, are added by hand.

Opposite below and right
Theorems can be produced by combining several separate stencils to build up an image. This is simple to do, as long as the paint is used sufficiently sparingly, and can produce lovely results.

THEOREM STENCILLING

Pictures composed by using several separate stencils to create an illusion of form are known as theorems. Theorems came into vogue in the early nineteenth century and were popular in both England and America. As with japanning, booklets of instruction were quickly available and it appears to have been a pastime that appealed equally to men and women.

Though the surviving theorems have often aged to a delicious peachy colour they were initially done on white or cream-coloured velvet. Once completed they were hung in frames like any conventional still-life painting.

This kind of stencilling can be done on any flat surface, and with any kind of paint, provided that it is used sufficiently sparingly. Since it is a more time-consuming process than simply stencilling patterns, it is advisable to choose a small area – a cushion cover, the panels of a door or cupboard are ideal.

OVERLAPPING BORDER

CIRCULAR CUSHION

This border is made up of a single stencil which is printed to overlap the previous print. To do this successfully use only a minute amount of paint on the brush and apply it to the edges of the stencil letting it fade out altogether in the middle and at the end where the next overlap will go. Corners can be negotiated by simply turning the overlapping print once or twice.

FLOWERS AND LEAVES

SQUARE CUSHION

This is made up of seven separate stencils combined. The simplest way to do this is to start printing from one or two central points and radiate out from these. Print successive stencils up to the visible edge of the preceding print.

Raw silk cushions stencilled in a variety of ways, from theorems made up of seven stencils to a curved border of wood anemones. The overlapping leaf is also used in the bronze powder stencilling section.

Vivid colour and patterns combine together to produce a tapestry of stencilled effects.

FLOORS AND FLOOR-CLOTHS

Floors and floor-cloths were originally stencilled as a poor man's alternative to rugs and carpets. Now stencilling can be appreciated in its own right. Though both will receive plenty of wear and tear, with sufficient varnishing a durable surface can be created that will withstand the passage of time.

Floors should be stencilled when all the preparatory work of sanding, painting or staining has been completed and one coat of varnish has been applied to the floor to prevent the paint from sinking into the wood should a mistake occur. (Refer to page 145 for preparation and finishes.) Floors should always be measured out from the centre point, found by crossing two diagonals from corner to corner; the pattern should radiate out from this, even if exact measuring is not essential.

Floor-cloths are made of heavyweight cotton duck, preferably twelve or fifteen ounce, which is generally available in craft or upholstery shops. Allow enough material to have a selvedge of three inches around the edge, which should be left unprimed. The rest of the material should be pinned or stapled out flat while the initial coats of paint are applied, otherwise it will not lie perfectly flat on the floor. A door, wall or a frame for stretching canvas are adequate for this.

Prime the surface with a mixture of emulsion paint and PVA (or Elmer's Glue All) adhesive to give the surface greater flexibility, tint this to the shade required for the background. Stipple the paint well into the weave of the canvas to build up a flat smooth surface. When the first coat is dry, sand it lightly and apply a second, sand this again before stencilling. When the stencilling is complete seal the surface with several coats of dilute PVA, finally applying one coat of matt varnish to cut the glossy finish of the PVA. When this is dry turn it over. Sand the back lightly to remove the bobbles of paint that will have come through from the first application of paint. Using PVA, glue down the edges, making a neat corner as the illustration shows. This may need weighting down at the corners while it dries. When it is dry sew or glue a backing onto it; this can consist of another layer of canvas or carpet felt.

As the surface becomes worn further layers of varnish can be applied. Always pick the floor-cloth up by rolling it loosely, if it is folded or crushed the paint layers will crack.

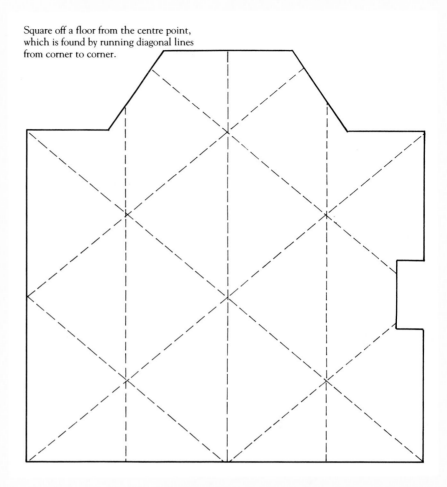

Square off a floor from the centre point, which is found by running diagonal lines from corner to corner.

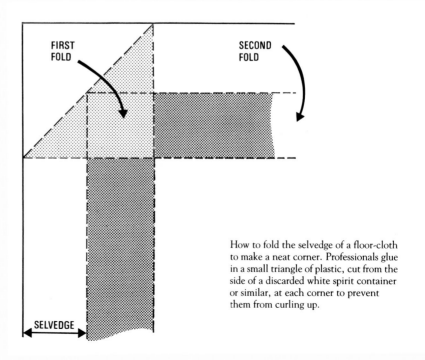

How to fold the selvedge of a floor-cloth to make a neat corner. Professionals glue in a small triangle of plastic, cut from the side of a discarded white spirit container or similar, at each corner to prevent them from curling up.

A pretty corn pattern stencilled inside a wide border onto a painted floor.

Opposite
This floor-cloth is decorated with a variety of paint finishes, discussed in a subsequent chapter, and stencilled with the pasque-flower border. It is protected with four coats of varnish. In front of the Aga it gets plenty of wear and tear but is durable and easy to clean.

DESIGNING STENCILS

Nothing quite matches the excitement of printing out your own stencils for the first time. No matter how much experience you have as a designer or draughtsman, there is still an element of surprise involved when the first proof is taken. Often it is only when a drawing is actually made into a stencil that its full design potential is revealed.

As well as basing stencils on an observation of the natural world, as we have done in this book, they can also be designed by adapting imagery and patterns from a vast array of sources and cultures. An ability to draw is useful, but by no means essential since copying, tracing, and taking rubbings are equally valid ways of assembling images. Ceramics and textiles are often particularly rich sources of inspiration needing little adapting to make a stencil. Pictures, photographs and line drawings generally translate badly into stencilled images, as detail and form are greatly reduced in the simplicity of the stencilling process. Stencils have their own inherent logic, which will determine the appropriateness of the image to the medium.

Generally, if you have not already formed an idea of a design, the existing decorative features of any room will provide the basis for a stencil.

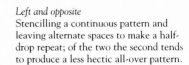

Left and opposite
Stencilling a continuous pattern and
leaving alternate spaces to make a half-
drop repeat; of the two the second tends
to produce a less hectic all-over pattern.

Below
Asymmetrical designs create fluid
patterns that suggest movement.
Symmetrical ones tend to be static and
less naturalistic.

A motif from a curtain pattern or a rug, a
particular part of a plate decoration or the
leaves and flowers from a thriving house-plant,
all offer plenty of scope for adaptation. If these
fail to inspire, illustrated children's books or
even patterns on the most mundane household
items can trigger the imagination.

PLAYING ABOUT WITH DESIGN

Simplicity in stencil design is usually one of the
keys to its success. A simple shape used
imaginatively can produce delightful results.
Creating movement is the other important
element in designing, and it is generated not
only by what is included in the design, but also
by the spaces between the individual parts of it.
As the illustration shows, repeating a pattern at
half-drop intervals, rather than continuously,
creates a fluid pattern that is not over-busy to
look at.

As a general rule, asymmetrical designs
suggest movement, fluidity and naturalism,
while a uniform distribution of even colour and
a symmetrical structure create a static, stylized
effect.

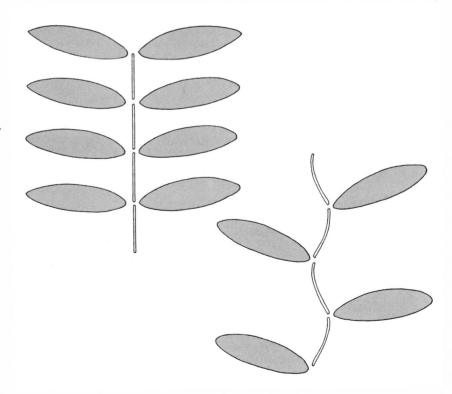

Start experimenting in design by cutting a stencil from a single motif that can be printed at random. If you plan to print it from alternate sides, cut two identical stencils. Play around with the design on some paper, changing the spacing and the layout several times until all the possible variations have been tried. The illustration demonstrates some of the different layouts that are possible.

Printing a stencil like this from different sides is one of the simplest means of generating an overall pattern which contains enough movement to be absorbing to the eye.

Once the layout has been decided upon, a larger stencil can be cut that includes all the repeat elements. This can be used on flat areas leaving the smaller stencils for fitting into awkward spaces.

Numerous patterns created from one small stencil. Once you have found the pattern to use by playing around with the layout a larger stencil can be cut that incorporates several repeats.

A sense of individual form is not necessarily lost by cutting one stencil rather than overlaying several, as long as the lines and edges are used to express the differences succinctly.

INCORPORATING TIES IN DESIGN

Making a stencil out of any design reduces it to a flat outline. This is because of the necessity for ties or bridges in the stencil to maintain its shape. A suggestion of form can be conveyed either by overprinting the design with subsequent stencil plates, to remove the flattening effect of the ties, or by shading the paint carefully across the stencil. The illustration shows both these methods of printing.

Right and below right
Two ways of using ties to emphasize the
form of an image.

Right
Each of the lines on this drawing
indicates where there should be a tie on
the stencil.

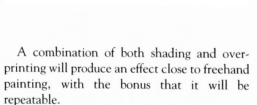

A combination of both shading and over-printing will produce an effect close to freehand painting, with the bonus that it will be repeatable.

Ties are part of a stencil's identity and generally, though they add to the flat quality of stencils, do not interfere with our perception of the overall image. Ties should be considered an inherent part of the stencil, and should be used, wherever possible, to enhance the design, rather than simply dividing up the cut areas. The leaf stencil illustrated has ties across it to suggest veining. As well as forming bridges across large open areas in a stencil, ties should also be used to prevent parts of the stencil from being vulnerable.

If part of the stencil has shapes cut away from it on three sides it will be easily damaged during cleaning and repositioning. With repeated use it will start to curl up, making a blurred print more likely. To prevent this from happening, examine your initial drawing and put in extra ties if they are necessary. Look at the illustration which demonstrates some of the ways in which ties can be introduced to designs in order for them to be successfully translated into stencils. Once all the ties have been drawn in it is advisable to shade, or do a rough cross-hatching on all the areas to be cut so there is a clear definition to follow.

Ties should be wide enough to do their job adequately. If the design requires areas that are very close together cut them in separate stencils, even if they are to be printed in the same colour.

Interpreting a watercolour, in this case
Edith Holden's pasque-flower to make a
stencil.

To produce the dense petals of a daisy head two stencils were cut.

Opposite
The daisy pattern used as a half-drop repeat on the wall and as a continuous pattern above the skirting board with a daisy-chain border around the window, makes a sweet decorative scheme for a child's room.

WHEN TO MAKE SEPARATE COLOUR PLATES

Separating a design into different colour plates allows for some wonderful effects that cannot be achieved with single stencils. It needs to be done in any design where contrasting colours adjoin, or where areas of colour overlap.

Separate colour plates require careful registration both in drawing out and in printing. This is relatively straightforward in transparent or semi-transparent stencils and can usually be done by eye as easily as with registration marks.

Registration marks should be made in permanent ink on acetate and pencil on plasticard or Mylar® paper. Opaque stencil card must have registration marks cut in it; choose two small parts of the design, and cut these same two parts in each colour plate. Refer to the chapter on **Materials and How to Use Them** for further information.

DESIGNING A BORDER

A design for a repeating border should be worked out on graph paper. This will ensure the repeat lines up perfectly without any obvious break in the design. Start by placing

Opposite and detail above
The poppy bunch and border co-ordinate together with Country Diary poppy material.

111

the preliminary drawing or rough outline of the border on the graph paper, leaving sufficient room either side for a repeat. Decide on the width of the repeat, a rough rule of thumb is that it should be twice the depth of the design, and mark it on the graph paper.

Copy the initial drawing onto tracing paper, and relocate it along the width of the repeat. This will provide two points of reference to work between.

It should then be relatively simple to fill in the remaining gap and to determine what the overall shape of the design will be like. Once the drawing is complete decide where the repeat point should be and mark it clearly. If the border is to go around a room it will save time to cut two repeats in one stencil.

COLOUR

Stencils are brought to life by their colours as much as their design. The colours in any stencil must work well together and combine harmoniously with the background colour in order to do the stencil justice. If a stencil is composed of several colours, they must be set in the same key, that is, equally brilliant or equally subdued. If one colour is stronger, or more vibrant, it will drown the other colours creating a flatter, two-dimensional effect. This means that the colours should be equal in tone, though they may vary in hue, to allow subtle colour ranges to hold their own.

Colours can be physically mixed together and applied in solid blocks or applied in layers while stencilling, to produce more vibrant optical colour mixes. Whichever method of mixing and applying paints you choose, remember colour is an infinitely adjustable thing, rather than an absolute that arrives in a tube. You can experiment and explore.

Though colour is largely a matter of taste and intuition, there are a few basic observations that need to be mentioned. Various terms used for describing colour, its effect on other colours and on the onlooker are also outlined here.

FUNDAMENTALS ABOUT COLOUR

Theoretically colours are derived from three primary colours: yellow, blue and red, plus black and white. Two of the three primaries are mixed to produced secondary colours:

yellow and blue = green
yellow and red = orange
blue and red = purple

The primary not used to produce the secondary colour is known as its complementary colour:

yellow complements purple
blue complements orange
red complements green

Variations of these complementary colours often work well together, enhancing each other's qualities without being subdued themselves.

Mixing a colour with a little of its complementary colour will subdue it without destroying it. Adding raw umber to any colour has the same effect. Mixing white to a colour will lighten it, as well as making it more opaque. Mixing black to a colour requires caution. It can alter the intensity of a colour as well as deepening the tone.

DESCRIBING EFFECTS OF COLOUR

How people respond to colour, and describe it, is largely subjective, but there are certain descriptive terms that are commonly used:
Hue – the main cast of a colour
Intensity – the strength or purity of a colour
Tone – lighter or darker versions of the same colour.
So two colours of different hue but the same tone would be equally powerful side by side, and would appear equally grey in a black and white photograph.

Colours are described as being warm or cool in relation to each other as well as occupying a spatial position, that is, advancing or retreating. The temperature of a colour is not necessarily a division into yellow, orange and red being warm and greens and blue being cool. An acid yellow could be described as sharp but cool, while a blue mixed with crimson could be warm in effect. Greys can be warm or cool depending on whether they have yellow, red or blue added to them. The very coolest grey is produced by mixing only black and white.

Our perception of colour is affected by surrounding or background colours. White tends to overpower small areas of colour, making them appear a uniform grey from a distance. Warmer tones, off-white, cream or apricot, tend to hold colours more successfully, as well as being easy colours to live with. A subtle paint finish, like ragging or stippling, can also create a pleasant background to stencils. Dark colours provide a dramatic setting, and can have the effect of throwing the stencils into relief. Colours for dark surfaces must be opaque to be clearly visible.

In this design the bow was the initial element. It was repeated at an interval of five inches on the graph paper and the connecting ribbon and flowers drawn in. Only one of the bows would be cut to make a stencil, the other would be traced for registration.

Opposite
Detail of the dog-rose border and swag, part of which has been stencilled in this dormer window.

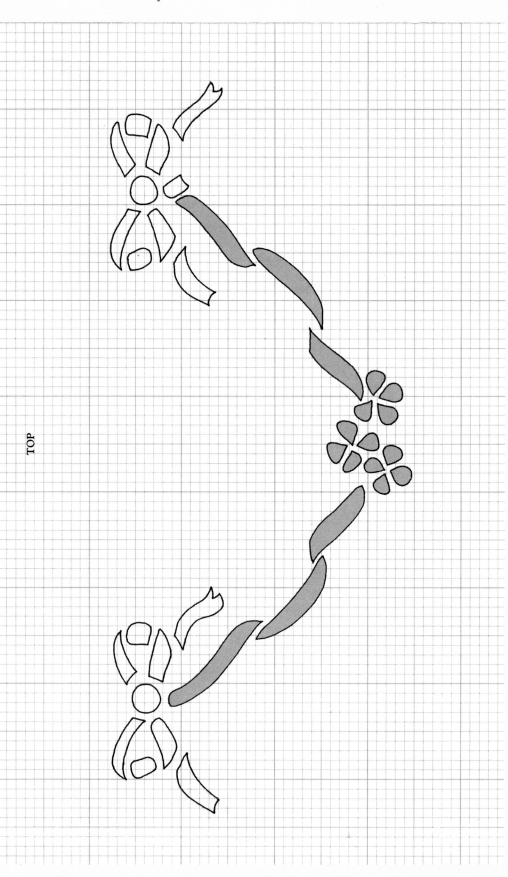

TOP

114

Detail of stencilled room shown on page 35 using the Purple Vetch stencil.

MIXING COLOURS

Mix colours in small quantities for preliminary colour matching, and work by adding darker colours to lighter ones. Add a little solvent, water or white spirit, with the new colour to enable it to mix easily, and make sure it is thoroughly stirred into the base colour. Some colours change on drying, so when matching colours exactly, let the test strip dry completely before adding more paint.

Recently, ready-mixed colours for stencilling have become available in sludgy subdued shades that contain a good deal of white opaque pigment. If you are using these, avoid mixing them beyond adding white or black.

Though it is generally considered to be good practice and training to begin with the basic primaries plus black and white, certain colours cannot be produced by mixing and need to be bought. Otherwise mixing colours for yourself is definitely worth pursuing, as a source of satisfaction as well as a means of increasing your colour awareness and discrimination.

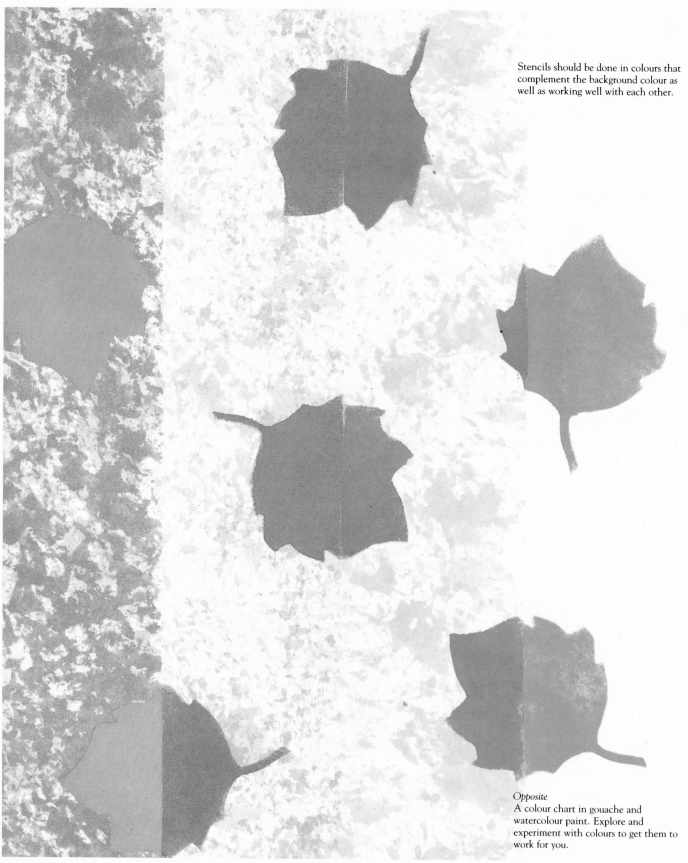

Stencils should be done in colours that complement the background colour as well as working well with each other.

Opposite
A colour chart in gouache and watercolour paint. Explore and experiment with colours to get them to work for you.

Decorative Paint Finishes

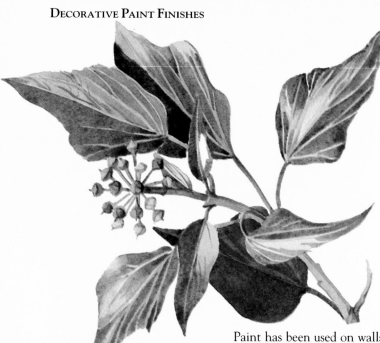

Paint has been used on walls and furniture as a means of both decorating and protecting for centuries. Using paint to imitate nature has a history that dates back to the ancient Egyptians. Until the advent of ready-made paints decorators knew how to combine ingredients and pigments to produce the right finish and colour. Learning to mix paint as well as learning the techniques different paint finishes require, necessitated a long apprenticeship.

Inevitably, to preserve and maintain standards of excellence, methods were jealously guarded and the traditional finishes of graining, marbling and gilding came to inspire a sort of awe in ordinary home decorators. Though these paint finishes are outside the scope of this book, they are within most peoples' capabilities and are a rewarding study in themselves.

The paint finishes described here are borrowed or simplified versions of old techniques coupled with a few modern variations. They are all suitable as backgrounds or adjuncts to stencilling, and like stencilling require only a little patience, care and enthusiasm to be achieved.

Purpose of Paint Finishes

Though the range of colours available in emulsion and oil paint has proliferated over recent years, the quality of the colour in a heavy opaque medium, makes for unrelievedly monochromatic interiors. Physically combining colour is only one way of producing colour mixes. If colour is applied separately to a surface in several transparent layers, the colours combine in the eye of the beholder, literally on the retina, to much greater effect. Colour, instead of being an absolute thing that arrives in a can, becomes infinitely variable and delightful. Colour glazes can be applied in

A range of brushes for decorative finishes, from right to left: a full size 6in × 4in stippling brush; a badger hair softener, used for clouding but invaluable for other faux finishes like graining and marbling; a dragging brush, also called a flogger (US walnut stippler); a dusting brush, a split-ended soft-bristled brush, used to clean surfaces prior to painting; 1in household paintbrush; oval varnishing brush.

many ways; they can be used to soften and disguise bad features or to highlight good ones.

Any one of the decorative paint finishes outlined in this book is within the scope of most people. Some finishes are better undertaken with the help of another person, some benefit from being practised on a piece of primed card before launching into entire rooms. However none of them requires any special artistic sensibility to achieve the desired effect.

MATERIALS AND EQUIPMENT FOR PREPARING SURFACES

Paint Stripper

This is useful for removing paint on fairly small areas, an item of furniture, or an inaccessible piece of moulding. The alkaline-based variety is extremely powerful, it should be applied with a synthetic brush as it dissolves natural bristle. Care should be taken to remove it thoroughly with several washes of water and vinegar to neutralize its action before applying subsequent paint layers. The oil-based variety is more expensive but safer to use and more controllable. Always use paint stripper according to the manufacturer's instructions, wear protective gloves, and cover the surrounding area.

Blowlamps, Blowtorches and Electrical Paint Strippers

These all serve the same purpose of softening the paint so it can be scraped off the surface by heating it. Care should be taken to avoid scorching the wood beneath.

Scrapers

Flexible blades of varying widths can be used to scrape paint off flat surfaces. Use a shave hook for mouldings and recesses. These come with a straight-sided triangular head or with one curved and one straight side.

Abrasives

These are useful at every stage of decorating, from preparation through to the final finish:

Sandpaper – the cheapest abrasive paper. It is available in three or four finishes from rough to smooth. It tends to clog and disintegrate quickly.
Garnet papers – these are more expensive and longer lasting than sandpaper.
Silicon Carbide papers – wet-and-dry papers

used for sanding down between coats of paint. They can be moistened with linseed oil or water to reduce dust in the atmosphere and improve the abrasive qualities.
Steel wool – this is available in several grades from coarse through to very fine. It is useful for reaching inaccessible recesses.

Powders and Polishes

Powdered pumice, or rottenstone which is finer, are traditionally used with lemon oil to create a final finish on furniture. Whiting, talcum powder or ordinary white flour can be used as substitutes. They are applied with a soft cloth and buffed to a shine.

Fillers

Use all-purpose cellulose or vinyl-based fillers for small cracks and defects in plaster or in walls. Deep cracks may need filling in several applications to ensure the filler dries and hardens thoroughly. It can be applied with an ordinary household or putty knife. Wiping the surface lightly with a damp cloth just before it hardens will save time sanding.

A strong all-purpose cleaner (such as sugar soap) should be used to wash down walls before painting to cut through any surface grease. It can also be used for washing out brushes.

All decorating requires some preparation. Defects in wood and plaster, chips in old layers of paint, tears in wallpaper – all these should be tackled before you start.

WALLS

Newly plastered walls must be left for two or three weeks to dry thoroughly before painting them. If they are going to be distempered they should be covered with two applications of HOT size to seal the surface. For other types of paint two coats of diluted emulsion will provide a seal.

Walls covered with a previous coat of paint should be wiped with a solution of sugar soap (or similar all-purpose cleaner) and water.

Sometimes irregularities in wall surfaces show up more clearly after one application of paint, so be prepared to do some more sanding if that is the case. Alternatively, hang lining paper to hide the worst defects. Lining paper is manufactured in three gauges or thicknesses. The heaviest gauge, which is like drawing paper, will work wonders in hiding irregularities.

A cottage Gothic feel in this delightful attic bathroom. It is sponged to conceal slight irregularities in the surface and stencilled with one part of the ivy border.

WOOD

New wood should have all the knots in it covered with knotting compound, a mixture of methylated spirits (denatured alcohol) and shellac, to prevent resin seeping out and discolouring the paint. It should then be primed with wood primer and undercoat. Follow this by sanding thoroughly before applying the base coat.

Previously painted wood should be sanded to provide a slightly roughened surface for the new paint to key into. Take particular care if the previous paint had a gloss finish, this must be cut through completely to provide a sound surface for the new paint. If the existing paint is badly chipped and uneven, it should be stripped with a proprietary paint stripper or a blowlamp.

Wood that has been French polished along with subsequent coats of wax polish, should be sanded with a fine grade of wire wool, 001 or 002, and then wiped down with methylated spirits. Leave it to dry before wiping again with a strong all-purpose cleaner, then follow the directions for new wood.

When any small cracks have been filled, smooth the surface. Wrap the sand paper around a small flat block of wood when sanding flat areas and sand in the direction of the grain. Use your sense of touch as much as sight to locate and remove any slight roughness in the surface.

BASE COAT

The base coat of paint is the one applied after the initial layers of priming and undercoating, but before any glaze or wash. Usually a minimum of two applications is necessary to provide a solid opaque colour to set off any subsequent glaze.

All the decorative paint finishes outlined here require a flat, that is, sheenless, base coat. It need not be oil-based, though oil-based paint is preferable on woodwork, as long as it completely seals the surface beneath it. Use flat white oil paint, available in specialist paint supply shops, or oil-based paint with an eggshell finish. These can be tinted with universal tinting colours, available at ordinary paint suppliers, or artist's oil colours.

Vinyl silk finish or ordinary emulsion paint can also be used to provide a base coat, more than one is advisable. They can be tinted with gouache or powder paint.

SEQUENCE OF PAINT

Usually water-based paints go on walls and oil-based paints go on wood, with the exception of certain water soluble wood primers. Oil-based glazes will go onto water-based paint successfully, while water-based washes tend to prove less durable on an oil-based surface. Some paint finishes can only be done in an oil-based glaze, a water-based one would dry too quickly.

Always ensure any surface is adequately sealed before applying a glaze, this is particularly important with walls. Otherwise the oil in the glaze will be absorbed leaving a patchy and unworkable surface.

A paint finish will reveal portions of the base coat of paint, so it should be tinted an appropriate shade. If you are planning to tint it yourself buy white paint, avoid using brilliant white as a base, it contains a lot of blue pigment.

Opposite
Detail of the ivy stencil in the dormer window of the bathroom.

An old neglected wall proves to have the charm of any contemporary paint finish, bordered with periwinkle.

TINTING PAINT

Tinting must be done with a pigment in a compatible medium! Use either artist's oils or universal stainers for all oil-based paints. Use gouache, acrylic or powder colours for water-based paints.

It is a good idea to make colour mixes before embarking on tinting gallons of paint – take note of the proportions needed to achieve certain colours. All colours should be diluted with their appropriate solvent before adding them to the paint. This enables them to be mixed easily. Add the pigment little by little, stirring it thoroughly into the paint. Make a colour sample on a piece of paper each time more pigment is added. Always add dark colour to light, it is much easier to deepen a colour than it is to lighten it.

Do not attempt to mix very deep shades for a base colour, these are more easily suggested by applying several coats of tinted varnish on top of a ready-mixed, deeply tinted base coat.

CHOOSING A PAINT FINISH

A paint finish will subtly underline the overall feeling of decoration in a room. Finishes like ragging and sponging create a homely, cosy effect and can usually be relied on to cover a multitude of defects, while dragging and stippling tend to draw attention to the surface and its relative perfection.

All of these techniques can be used as a basis for stencilling. Generally the broken areas of colour provided by something like ragging or stippling subdue the contrast made by a stencil, so that it blends into the overall surface.

PAINT RECIPES

OIL-BASED GLAZES

Home-Made Glazing Liquid
5 parts pure turpentine
3 parts boiled linseed oil – use artist's quality linseed oil to avoid the worst of the yellowing effects produced by low grade linseed oil
½ part oil driers – or according to manufacturer's recommendations
3 tablespoons whiting – available in hardware shops

Mix these ingredients together thoroughly. An oil glaze takes at least twelve hours to dry properly though it may be touch dry in six hours. Weather conditions will affect this and should be born in mind when mixing the glaze. More linseed oil will increase the drying time; oil driers will, to a certain extent, reduce it, but should be used according to the manufacturer's instructions.

Home-made glazing liquid is a thin, flat, transparent glaze. Apply it sparingly to vertical surfaces as it runs easily. More whiting can be added to give it a little exta body.

Scumble Glaze/Faux Finish Glaze

This is the name given to ready-made glazing liquid. It has the advantage over the home-made variety in that it is more viscous and therefore doesn't run on a vertical surface.

Some scumble glaze has a high linseed oil content and therefore it tends to yellow quickly, particularly in areas out of natural light. Blue and green tints can be badly affected if this happens, so it is worth looking for as clear a glaze as possible, they vary from one manufacturer to another. (See 'Suppliers'.)

Ready-made scumble glaze needs thinning with turpentine or white spirit (mineral spirit) before use, this also reduces the sheen of the glaze when it is dry.

Oil-Paint Glazes

Eggshell finish oil paint or flat oil paint can be reduced with two parts turpentine to one part linseed oil to make a more opaque glaze. It should be diluted to the consistency of single cream.

WATER-BASED WASHES

Distemper

The precursor of emulsion paint, distemper has been used on walls for centuries. This recipe does not produce a waterproof paint and its powdery quality tends to attract dust, but it has a flat, chalky finish that cannot be replicated by modern emulsions:

Size
Water
Whiting

Make up the size according to the manufacturer's instructions and leave it to set to a jelly-like consistency. Fill another container with cold water and add whiting until it forms a peak two to four inches above the surface. Leave this to

soak for at least one hour then stir and tint with water-based or powder paint. Heat the glue by placing its container into a bowl of hot water. When it is runny add it to the whiting mixture.

Use approximately equal parts of size mixture to whiting mixture, it should be the consistency of double cream. If it starts to thicken while you are using it place the container in hot water to thin it again. Distemper doesn't keep for more than two days and should be discarded after that time.

Apply distemper to the wall with a wide, long-bristled brush, using sideways brush strokes to prevent it running down the wall.

Oil-bound distempers and ready-mixed water-based ones are available in specialist paint shops. They generally produce a more resilient surface. All distemper may be diluted with water to make a wash for sponging or ragging.

Emulsion Glazes

Ordinary emulsion paint can be thinned with water and used as an opaque wash. It should be thinned to the consistency of double cream.

Very thin washes of transparent colour should always have a small amount of emulsion in them for body. The addition of a water-based sealant like corseal or PVA (or Elmer's Glue All) will make them more resilient.

APPLYING WATER-BASED WASHES

Water-based washes dry quickly. This makes them unsuitable for stippling or dragging, or any other technique that involves working into a wet glaze. When applying a wash, the critical part is in maintaining a wet edge. Work with as wide a brush as your wrist can support, four or five inches is comfortable for most people. Apply the wash with horizontal strokes to prevent too much of it pouring down the wall. Keep a large sponge handy to mop spills and runs, but ensure carpets and furniture are well protected before starting.

TECHNIQUES FOR APPLYING GLAZES

Sponging

This finish is created by applying colour with a marine sponge to produce an irregular series of marks reminiscent of the surface of the sponge. It is the easiest of all paint finishes, and can produce a beautiful dappled effect, particularly if several colours are applied.

Materials

A marine sponge, the larger it is the greater its covering capacity, but not less than three inches in diameter
Newsprint
A paint kettle, plate or bowl for holding the glaze
Step-ladder
Rubber gloves
Masking tape
Rags

Begin by making some samples on paper to determine the colours and their distribution. Usually the lightest colour is applied first, followed by more intermittent applications of darker tones. Once the colours have been selected mix up sufficient quantities of oil-based glaze or water-based wash. One litre will be ample for sponging a room eleven feet by twelve feet from ceiling to skirting.

Unless the woodwork is to be decorated it should be protected along its edge with strips of masking tape, as should light switches and other fixtures on the wall.

Dampen the sponge before use to soften it and squeeze it out between rags. This should be done even if you are using an oil-based glaze as the water will protect the centre of the sponge and prevent it from hardening when dry.

Dip the sponge into the glaze and dab it out on paper until an even series of marks form. You are then ready to start applying it to the wall. Avoid a regular pattern of marks building up but keep the density of the paint consistent. Using a different size sponge for subsequent colours prevents the sponge marks from becoming irritatingly regular.

Wash the sponge out at frequent intervals to prevent it from becoming over saturated, and wash it out thoroughly when you have finished.

Colours for sponging

Use close shades of the same colour to achieve a subtle effect. A limited application of a complementary colour in a similar tone can enhance the initial colour without being obtrusive.

Sponging Off

Sponges can also be used to lift a wet glaze off the surface, producing a more subtle, mottled effect than applying glaze with a sponge. Apply the glaze with a paint brush in a vertical band approximately two feet wide. Wet the sponge

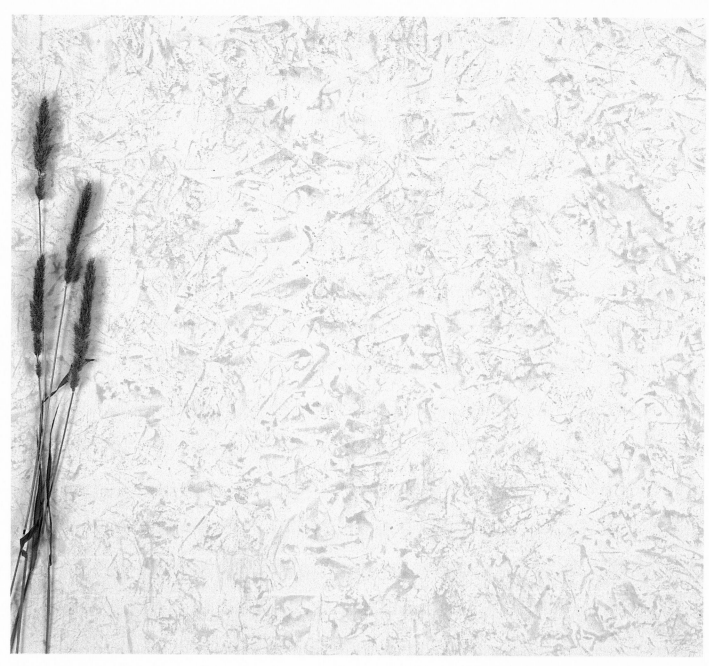

Ragging – applying paint with a rag rolled over the surface. This finish was done in a bay leaf green emulsion wash over a cream base.

to soften it and squeeze out any excess water by placing it in a dry towel. Dab the sponge into the glaze, lifting it out cleanly, without smudging the marks made. The sponge will quickly become saturated with glaze and need frequent cleaning. Always ensure it is as dry as possible before resuming, otherwise the marks will be uneven.

Ragging

Ragging can be done with any sort of lint-free rag or with a piece of chamois leather.

Depending on the size of the rag and the colour used it can produce diverse effects, from a watery softness, to a surface like marble.

Materials

Rags – any fabric will do, but natural fabrics are more absorbent than man-made ones, or a piece of chamois leather

Paint kettle to hold the glaze

Rubber gloves

Step-ladder

Newsprint

Take the dry rag and immerse it in the glaze. Squeeze out the excess glaze very thoroughly and then scrumple the rag or chamois into a wad or sausage shape, do not fold it neatly, it is the random folds that form the marks. Roll this out in different directions on the surface several times before refolding the rag. This is necessary to prevent a regular pattern from building up. When the rag needs reloading with glaze a small amount can be applied with a brush to one corner and worked into the rest of the rag.

Subsequent colours can be applied using rags of different material to produce a contrasting effect.

Ragging Off

Dry rags can be used to remove a wet glaze. Apply the glaze in vertical bands approximately two feet wide with an ordinary paintbrush. Then take a dry rag, have a large supply of them to hand, scrumple it up and roll it into the wet surface, refolding it from time to time to prevent a discernible pattern from emerging. Discard the rag when saturated with paint.

Ragging off – a blue scumble glaze broken up by using dry rags rolled into the wet surface.

131

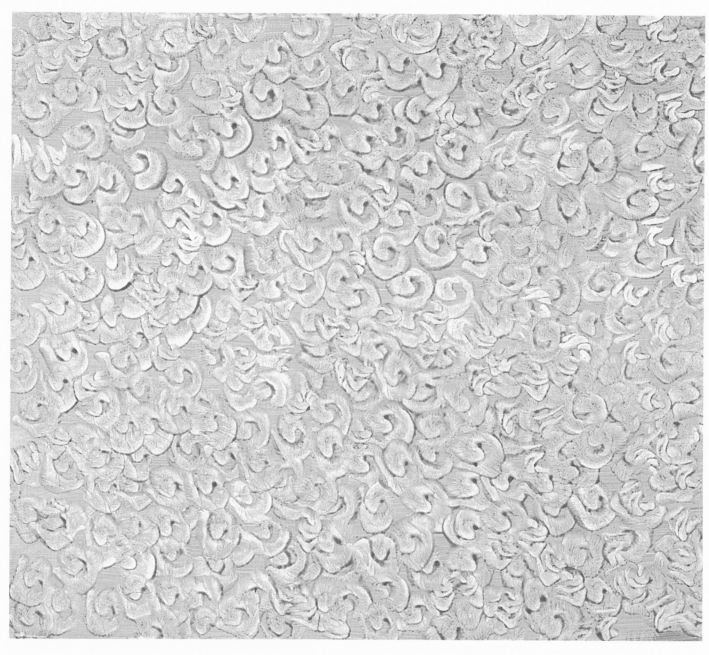

A small spiral of Plasticene pressed into a wet glaze produced this finish.

Opposite
A box lined with an oil glaze. Plasticene was pressed into it to make this pattern.

Besides rags there are a variety of things that can be used to break up a wet-glazed surface. Plastic bags of different thicknesses will produce more distinctive marks than ragging. Lightweight paper can also be used. Actual newsprint should be avoided as the ink will muddy the colours.

Plasticine (or similar modelling substance) can be made into shapes and pressed into wet glaze to produce extraordinary patterns. Leaves and even vegetables can be used to make marks in the surface. Only the scale of the area being painted need limit your ingenuity.

Dragging

Dragging a wet glaze undoubtedly produces one of the most elegant paint finishes. It can be done on any surface that has been prepared to a fine smooth finish. Thorough preparation is essential as any irregularities in the surface tend to become more, rather than less, pronounced once the glaze has been dragged.

Dragging is done with a long-bristled brush, traditionally a 'flogger' or dragging brush. This is pulled through the wet glaze to create a series of fine parallel lines. The flogger brush derives its name from its use in graining techniques

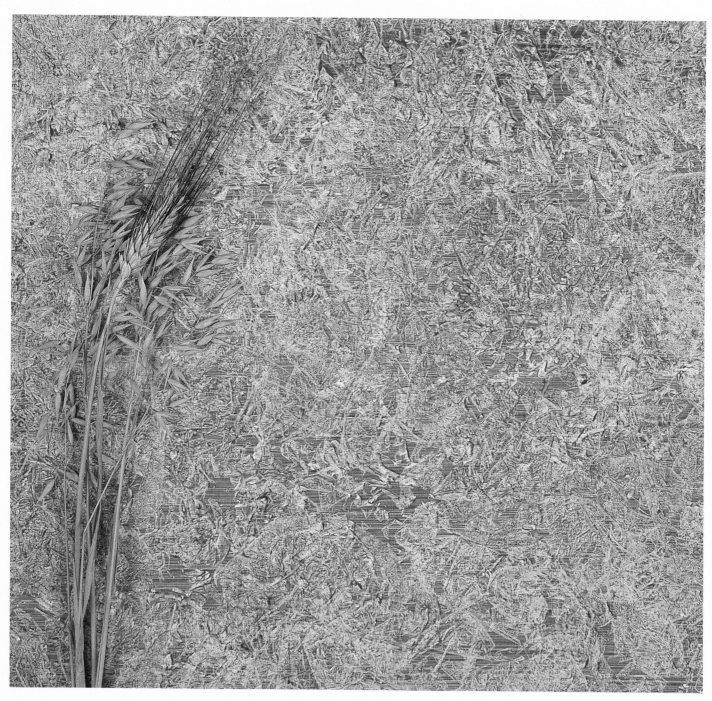

Bagging – plastic bags pressed or rolled into a wet glaze create a surprisingly distinctive finish.

where the wet glaze is struck or flogged with the brush to produce a mottled surface reminiscent of wood.

Dragging is usually associated with the twentieth-century designer and decorator John Fowler, who pioneered a revival of decorative paint finishes. A fine example of dragged woodwork, in a raspberry-coloured glaze over a buff-coloured base coat, is also found in Brighton Pavilion.

Materials

Dragging brush, or a long-bristled three-inch household paintbrush or a varnishing brush
Paint kettle for holding the glaze
Household paintbrush for initial application of glaze
Roller, sponge or acrylic fibre (optional)
Supply of clean rags

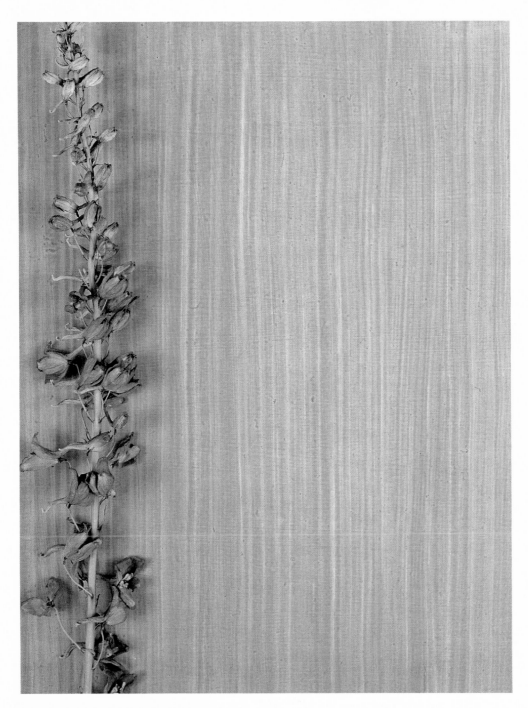

Dragging Woodwork

Apply the glaze evenly with a brush. It should be applied in a sufficiently small area to ensure it can be dragged before it dries. Follow this application by rolling the surface with the dry roller to remove any trace of brush marks and ensure the glaze is evenly distributed. Then dip the dragging brush about half an inch into the glaze and wipe it on a clean rag. This will prevent the first line of dragging from removing a disproportionate amount of glaze. Start dragging the glazed surface in a steady even movement, always following the direction of the grain. Wipe the brush on a dry rag after each successive line of dragging to prevent it from becoming saturated with glaze.

Dragging need not follow the direction of the grain in areas where it is being used to suggest a veneer or inlay on a box, tray or similar item.

Dragging – a delphinium blue dragged over a pale blue base.

Radiators should be given the same treatment as the rest of the wall to prevent them from being too intrusive. This one has been rag-rolled.

Preceding pages
A Georgian dining-room dragged in a dusty blue over a pale grey base coat. Trompe panels were painted in to underline the proportions of the room after the walls had been dragged. A small stencil of grapes and wheat above the dado rail echoes the pattern of the cornice.

Dragging Walls

Dragging a wall poses more of a challenge than dragging wood simply by virtue of its scale. It is advisable to work with someone else, if an entire room is going to be dragged: one to apply the glaze and the other to drag it.

Apply the glaze in vertical bands, approximately two feet wide, smoothing it with the roller to remove extraneous brush marks. Hang a plumb line ahead of the area that you are dragging to provide a true vertical with which to align your brush.

The brush can be dragged down from the top and up towards the middle to meet at a halfway point on the wall. Unless there is a dado rail, or you are planning to stencil a border over the top, this meeting point should vary in height around the room or it will stand out as a conspicuous dividing point.

A second dragging can also be done at right angles to the first to produce a woven texture.

Colours for dragging
Dragging presents delightful opportunities for

the interaction of colour. The base coat can be given a lustrous depth and finish by dragging in a transparent glaze of the same shade but several tones deeper. Other effects include creating colour mixes by dragging in a different colour, for instance, blue over green; or a complementary colour, for instance, terracotta red over pale bay-leaf green; or dragging in a much lighter colour than the base coat.

Stippling

Stippling is one of the most subtle of paint finishes. It should be virtually imperceptible when seen across a room, but nevertheless will create a discreet bloom of colour that enhances the atmosphere of any room.

It is done by lightly pressing a short-bristled brush into a wet glaze to produce a series of small marks. This is harder work than it sounds.

On small areas, below a dado rail or on woodwork, stippling can be done with a dusting brush, or clothes-brush, but to stipple an entire room invest in a full-size stippling brush.

Dragging – here the same yellow base coat has two different glazes dragged over it.

Stippling – a blue glaze stippled over a forget-me-not blue base coat.

Opposite
Clouding – two shades of ultramarine blue glaze have been used over a white base to make this clouded panel.

Materials
4-inch household paintbrush for applying the glaze
Paint kettle or bowl to hold the glaze
Roller, either foam or acrylic fibre (optional)
Clean rags
Stippling brush or equivalent
Apply the glaze evenly with the paintbrush in vertical sections approximately two feet wide on walls, or wider if only a portion of the wall is being stippled. Go over this with the dry roller to remove any brush marks.

Stipple the glaze with the brush in a short jabbing movement, working evenly over the entire area. Keep a cloth dampened with a little turpentine on hand to wipe the brush at frequent intervals to prevent it from becoming saturated with glaze.

Colours for stippling
Strong colour contrasts tend to show up any unevenness in the stippling and should be avoided. The most successful effects are created by stippling in tones close to the colour of the base coat.

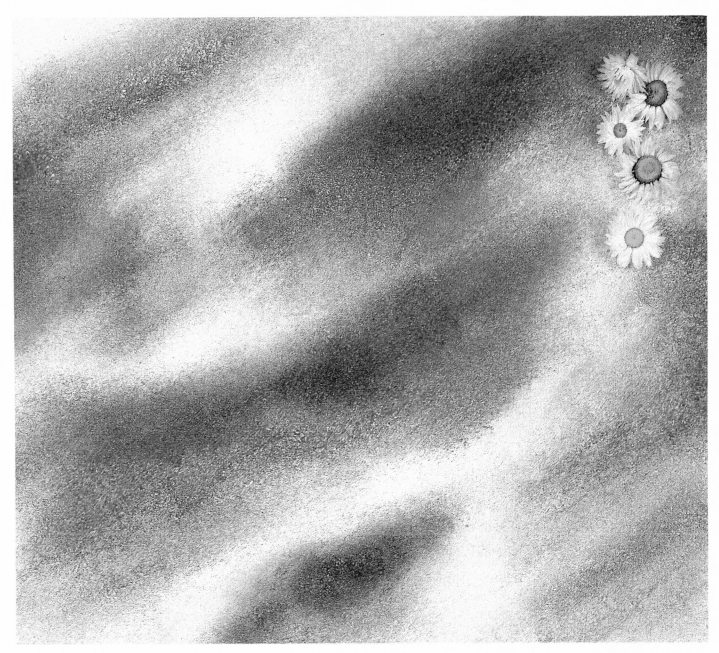

Clouding

As its name suggests this technique aims to produce something of the soft dappled effect of cloudy skies. Popular in the Twenties and Thirties, it was commonly done on ceilings, sometimes within a border, and usually in shades of blue and sometimes rosy pink. It can be done in several stages to build up a surface with great depth and luminosity.

Materials

Ready-made scumble glaze thinned 20% with turpentine

2-inch household paintbrush

Plates or paint kettles for holding the glaze, or glazes

Dusting brush or badger hair softener or soft lint-free rags

Apply the glaze in irregular patches, or in roughly parallel broken lines, with the paintbrush. The glaze should be viscous enough to remain in place and can be left for up to two hours. It should then be worked into with the badger or dusting brush, or cloth made into a pad shape. The glaze should be teased out

141

gently so that some of the edges are softened completely, leaving other areas almost untouched. Keep a cloth moistened with turpentine, on hand to wipe the brush clean from time to time.

Leave this to dry for at least twenty-four hours. Subsequent coats can be applied and worked into in the same way. Though the basic way of applying the glaze should be maintained, ie patches or parallel lines, the subsequent coats of glaze can be applied over different areas.

DECORATIVE FINISHES FOR FLOORS

Floors receive the greatest wear and tear of any surface so it is worth taking time and trouble to paint and protect them in the right way if they are not going to be carpeted. Old floor-boards, particularly if they are pine, can turn an unpleasant yellow colour after the necessary coats of varnish have been applied, while proprietary floor paints, though tough, are only manufactured in a limited range of colours and one glossy finish. This kind of paint cannot be painted over easily and should be removed by sanding before applying different coats of paint.

NEW FLOOR-BOARDS

Lightening floor-boards

Floor-boards can be lightened by scrubbing them with a weak solution of household bleach and water. Make sure you wear protective gloves and clothing while working. Bleaching will reduce the tendency of pine to yellow and also remove any scuff marks which often occur in the tender surface of new wood. When the floor had dried go over it lightly with sandpaper to smooth off any irregularities in the surface. If the wood is to be stained this is the point at which to do it. Use a proprietary woodstain, like Sadolin, or mix up your own using equal parts of linseed oil and turpentine tinted with artist's oil paint. One litre of this should cover a floor approximately ten feet by thirty feet. Alternatively the floor can be darkened slightly by rubbing it with pure turpentine.

Leave the woodstain to dry for twenty-four hours before applying a coat of varnish. The initial coat can be diluted up to thirty per cent with turpentine. Any stencilling or freehand painting should come at this point. When these are dry, varnish the floor with a minimum of five coats for thorough protection.

OLD FLOOR-BOARDS

These must have the gaps caulked and the nails countersunk before being sanded with an industrial sander, which can be hired from most home decorating shops. Use an edging sander to get at all the awkward areas.

Remove all furniture from a room before sanding it, and work with the door closed and protected with a dust sheet, otherwise fine sawdust will invade the whole house.

After sanding seal the floor with some sort of varnish immediately unless it is going to be stained, bleached or painted.

Paint Glazes for Lightening Floors

A glaze of flat or eggshell oil-based paint, diluted to a runny consistency with two parts turpentine to one part linseed oil can be used as an effective way of lightening floor-boards without obscuring the grain of the wood. The glaze can be tinted with raw umber to produce a dirty off-white, or warmed with a little burnt sienna, or made a cool grey with the addition of Payne's grey or lamp black. Whatever the colour, it should not be in too great a contrast to the underlying colour of the boards.

Apply the glaze with a three-inch paintbrush along the length of one or two floor-boards. Leave it for about ten minutes and then go back to the starting point and with a clean rag wipe off the glaze. This will leave some colour in the surface of the wood but not enough to obscure the quality of the grain. Leave it to dry and then apply a thinned coat of varnish before stencilling or painting further.

Cissing or Fossilstone Marbling

Wonderful naturalistic effects can be achieved with this technique. Sometimes it is used as an adjunct to more conventional marbling techniques, but it works well on its own. It can be done on vertical surfaces but begin by experimenting on a floor, perhaps masking the edges and using it as part of a border design.

Colours for fossilstone marbling

The most successful colours are naturalistic, earth shades on a buff or grey base coat. More flamboyant fantastic effects can be produced by strongly contrasting the base coat and the glaze and perhaps introducing touches of gold and silver powder. Avoid using more than two, or at the most three, different coloured glazes.

Preceding page, left
Detail of the floor-cloth. After the surface had been prepared the centre rectangle and edge were masked off and fossilstoned and dragged respectively. The intervening border was rag-rolled before being stencilled.

Preceding page, right
Detail of antiqued mirror.

Opposite
Detail of painted and stencilled dresser-top.

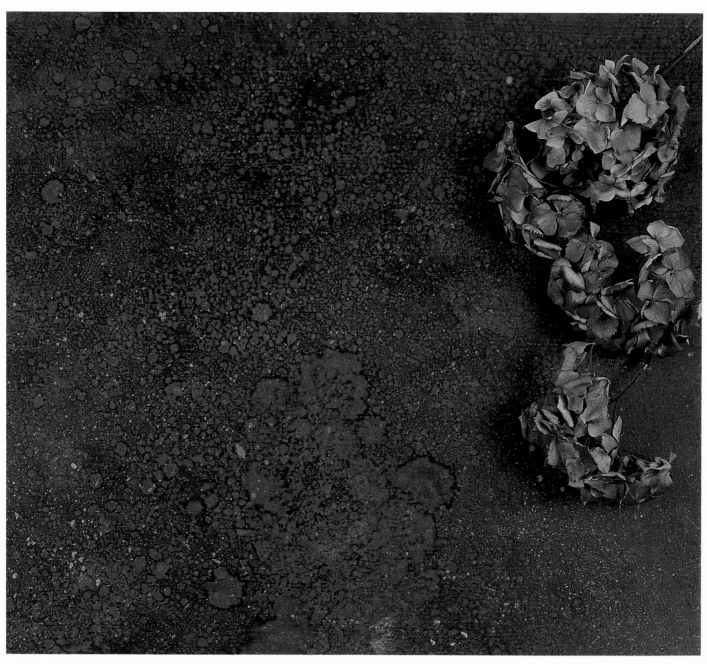

Fossilstone marbling in a bottle green glaze with a spattering of gold flecks over an evergreen base. This rich dense surface makes an ideal finish for decorating floors.

Materials
Oil-based glazes
Linseed oil
Rags
Sponge
2 old toothbrushes or ½-inch paintbrushes with short bristles
Turpentine
Methylated spirit
Bronze powders (optional)
Prepare the surface by priming with at least two coats of the base paint, sanding well between

coats. When dry mark out the divisions of the surface with chalk and a set square. Mask off areas not being worked on with newspaper and masking tape. Ensure the masking tape is flush to the edge of the division.

The glaze is made by diluting either oil-based eggshell paint to the consistency of single cream with two parts turpentine to one part linseed oil, or diluting scumble glaze with turpentine for transparent glazes. Tint these to the required colour using artist's oils.

Before applying these wipe the primed

surface with a tack rag to remove any particles of dust. Then put a few drops of linseed oil onto a clean rag and wipe this over the surface, rather like greasing a baking tray. It will leave a faintly perceptible sheen to the surface and will allow the turpentine to bite into the glaze.

The surface is now ready for the glaze. This should be applied with a two-inch paintbrush in patches rather than a uniform cover. Subsequent colours should be applied in smaller patches. When this is done take a dry rag or sponge and blot the glaze so there are no

obvious edges where the colours meet and there are no remaining brush marks.

On a clean brush take up some turpentine. Dab it onto a rag to remove the excess. Hold it about twelve inches from the surface and draw your thumb or first finger across it to release a spray of turpentine onto the wet glaze. After a moment it will move the glaze into circles and dots. Wait until this movement is complete before spraying on more turpentine otherwise the whole thing will turn into a puddle of paint and solvent.

Sponging in two shades of pink over a white base and stencilled with a single leaf turned at random.

Equipment for stencilling a floor. The willow border has been cut as a repeat and as a single element so it can be used to make a variety of patterns. These new floor-boards were stained with a grey-green woodstain and given one protective coat of varnish before stencilling started.

Take up some methylated spirits on another brush and spray this onto the glaze. It will create a slightly different effect.

A small amount of pigment can be mixed with the turps, or try adding a little bronze powder to the methylated spirit. Any mistakes, huge drops of turpentine or runs, can be mopped up with kitchen towel.

When a sufficient amount of solvent has been added leave the whole thing to dry. This may take some time, twenty-four hours or longer. When it is quite dry, varnish it with a minimum of two coats of varnish, on floors a minimum of five coats.

ANTIQUING EFFECTS FOR FURNITURE

The term 'antiquing' covers a vast range of techniques that have been invented to replicate something of the charm that age and constant use confer on old pieces of furniture. Decadent though it may seem, antiquing is not a modern invention. Certain types of Japanese lacquer were created to look worn as early as

the fourteenth century, as were cracklure glazes, in imitation of old layers of paint. In Europe the habit of underpainting objects in a contrasting or complementary colour was a deliberate attempt to enhance the piece as the top coat was gradually chipped and worn away with time and the base began to show through.

Though antiquing can include the heavily physical, knocking and hitting pieces with mallets, chains and chisels, the ideas outlined here are solely concerned with the effects that can be produced with glaze and varnish. This ensures the results are subtle and any mistakes can easily be rectified.

Antiquing should be done with restraint and an eye for the overall logic of a piece. It may require a little observational research into how and where paint surfaces become worn and deteriorate. Inconsistencies in the final finish as well as exaggerated effects, tend to look theatrical and out of place.

Begin by choosing something small and definitely not valuable on which to practice different effects. Picture frames, small boxes or

Sponging in a single colour in an emulsion wash provides a textured background for stencilling.

Sponging in a blue-grey emulsion (above left) over a light blue base coat. On the right an emulsion crackle glaze has been used between the base coat and the succeeding coat of palest grey emulsion. This acts as a rapid drying agent causing the top coat to craze as it dries.

trays are ideal objects, but even a piece of skirting board, particularly if it has a moulded edge can be a good starting point. If you are working on a surface that is painted or stencilled, one or two coats of white shellac applied before you begin any antiquing will provide protection to the paint beneath.

ANTIQUING WITH VARNISH

The quickest way of creating an antique glaze is by adding a squeeze of raw umber artist's oil paint to a varnish, preferably one with a matt finish. It should be just enough to tint the

varnish a clear mousy grey.

As with all varnishing, the first stroke of the loaded brush should be applied to the middle of the surface and then brushed out to the edge. This will reduce the chances of drips and runs. Lay off the brush strokes in the same direction as the previous coat of paint. Drips or runs that are not mopped up while varnishing can be carefully removed with a craft knife blade when the surface has dried thoroughly.

This varnish can be left to dry before applying a further protective coat or it can be wiped off with a lint-free cloth about fifteen

On the left sponging off: an oil-based glaze broken up by pressing a marine sponge into the wet surface. On the right the same blue-grey emulsion as used on the previous page but sponged over a different base coat. Here the grey appears much more blue because of its proximity to a complementary colour.

minutes after being applied. This should be done on all the exposed areas of the object, leaving the tinted varnish in the recessed parts to emphasize their depth. It will also accentuate the brush marks in the previous coat of paint.

Raw umber has the effect of softening the bright newness of colours without dulling them, rather as the passage of time might affect them. However, the varnish can be tinted with other colours that can also be applied and then partially removed to produce more delicate effects. The varnish could be tinted a slightly deeper shade of the base coat, or perhaps a contrasting shade, vermilion over a buff or light green, pink over grey, magenta over blue and so on.

If wiping the wet varnish removes too much of it, if for instance it is being applied to a completely flat surface, then leave it to dry. The finest grade of wire wool 000 can then be rubbed over it to take it back to the base coat in those areas that would receive the greatest wear.

Always remember that a coat of varnish that has been wiped or sanded is not adequate

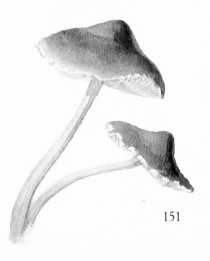

protection in itself, one or two further coats of varnish must be applied.

ANTIQUING WITH PAINT

Paint or a paint glaze can be applied in a similar way to varnish, that is, applied to the surface and then wiped off before it dries, leaving parts of it in recessed areas.

A very broad effect can be achieved by applying paint to the edges and/or the most prominent parts of an item as a quick way of highlighting form. This can be applied with an ordinary paintbrush but should then be softened well at the edges with a badger brush or dusting brush to create a blurred effect.

If the top layer of paint is going to be cut back in places to the base coat then there should be an intervening layer of varnish or shellac to protect the base coat from being accidentally removed.

Generally a fine grade of wire wool is used to remove the top coat around the areas that would be exposed to the greatest wear. A coarser effect is produced if this is done before the paint is completely dry. The wire wool should be rubbed along the grain or in the same direction as the preceding coat of paint.

SPATTERING

Spattering provides a subtle means of emphasizing form as well as suggesting the action of time. On small pieces the spattering fluid can be applied with an old toothbrush, otherwise an old household paintbrush with the bristles cut down to approximately half an inch in length will be adequate.

Spattering fluid can be bought ready-made or it can be prepared by diluting tinted varnish with white spirit and adding a little gold size. Alternatively black or sepia drawing ink can be used diluted with water.

Load the brush very sparingly and dab it on a dry rag to remove any excess fluid. Release the spray by drawing your first finger or thumb over the bristles in a slow even movement from a distance of six or nine inches.

Move your hand as you release the spray to prevent the spatter marks from having an obvious direction. Wipe your fingers frequently to avoid paint accumulating on them and dropping onto the surface.

Blotting with a paper towel leaves a series of small rings. A subsequent spattering with turpentine will produce a softer, more blurred effect. The paint dries almost at once so different colours can be applied immediately.

Dark colours should be applied sparingly, otherwise the end result is too dramatic. Any unwanted or misplaced spatters can be removed with a fine grade of wire wool after they have dried. A protective layer of varnish should be applied after spattering is completed.

FURTHER READING

Ayers, J *British Folk Art*
Overlook Press, NY 1977

Ayers, J *Shell Book of the Home in Britain*
Faber and Faber, London 1981

Bishop, A and Lord, C *The Art of Decorative Stencilling*
Thames and Hudson, London 1976

Blakemore, F *Japanese Design through Textile Patterns*
Weatherhill, NY 1978

Brazer, ES *Early American Decoration*
Pond Ekburg, NY 1940

Graysmith B *Wallpaper*
Studio Vista, London 1976

Jones, O *The Grammar of Ornament*
Bestseller, London 1986

Jennings, AS and Rothery, GC *The Modern Painter and Decorator*
3 Volumes, Caxton, London 1927

Lipman, J and Meulendyke, E *Techniques in American Folk Decoration*
Dover, NY 1972

Nakano, E and Stephan B *Japanese Stencil Dyeing*
Weatherhill, NY 1982

The Practical Home Decorator and Repairs Illustrated
Odhams, London 1952

O'Neil, I *The Art of the Painted Finish*
Morrow, NY 1971

Speltz, A *Styles of Ornament*
Dover, NY 1959

Stalker, J and Parker, G *A Treatise of Japanning and Varnishing*
London 1688, Academy edition, London 1971

V and A *Ornate Wallpapers*
V and A *Rococo Silks*
Webb and Bower/Michael Joseph, Exeter 1985

Waring, J *Early American Stencils on Walls and Furniture*
Dover, NY 1968

Wood, M *The English Medieval House*
Bracken Books, London 1983

SUPPLIERS

JW Bollom and Co Ltd
13 Theobalds Road
London WC1X 8SN

Quality household paint

Bricoprint
55–7 Glengall Road
London SE15 6NQ

All types of fabric paint, including metallic and
pearlized finishes

Craig and Rose
Princes Road
Dartford
Kent DA2 6EE

All supplies for decorative paint finishes

Cornelissen and Son Ltd
105 Great Russell Street
London WC1B 3RY

Bronze powders; pure pigments; fabric paint

Heffer and Co Ltd
24 The Pavement
Clapham
London SW4

Decorative artist's brushes of all types

Keep, JT and Sons Ltd
15 Theobalds Road
London WC1

General decorator's supplies

Ploton, E (sundries) Ltd
273 Archway Road
London N6

Metallic foils; cracklure mixtures; powdered pumice
and rottenstone

Potmolen Paints
Woodcock Industrial Estates
Warminster
Wilts

Paint supplies, especially good-quality distemper

Russell and Chapple Ltd
23 Monmouth Street
London WC2

Fine artist's linen, cotton duck of different weights,
calico

Caroline Warrender
1 Ellis Street
Lower Sloane Square
London SW1

All stencilling materials and pre-cut stencils

AMERICAN SUPPLIERS

West Coast

Daniel Smith Inc
4130 1st Ave South
Seattle
Washington 98134

All fine art supplies, mail order catalogue

Sid Moses Equipment and Tools
10456 Santa Monica Boulevard
LA
Calif 90025

Importers of Hamilton & Co decorative art brushes

Illinois Bronze Paint Co
Lake Zurich
Illinois 60047

Faux finish glaze

East Coast

Pearl Paint
308 Canal Street
NY NY 10013
Tel 0101 212 4317932

Fine art materials

New York Central Art Supply
62 Third Avenue
NY NY 10003 473-7715
Tel 0101 212 6856093

Fine art materials

NY Art Glass
PO Box 265
Hartsdale
NY 10530

Importers of Hamilton & Co decorative art brushes

Stencil Decor
Plaid Enterprises Inc
Box 7600
Norcross
GA 30091

Stencil crayons and pre-cut stencils

Stencil Index

INDEX

Acknowledgements

We would like to acknowledge the following people for contributing in various ways to the preparation of this book:

John Barker – designer craftsman
Malcolm Couch – line drawings
Anne-Marie Ehrlich – picture research
Alyson Gregory – editor
Charles Parsons – photography
Ron Pickless – design, additional line drawings
Martin Robertson – historical clues
Peter Wadham Antiques – props

For permission to photograph their houses:
P13 Diana Woolner
P 14, 15 Mr and Mrs Tibor
P 136, 137 David & Farough Sherlock-Thomas

All country diary stencils photographed by Charles Parsons except:
P 81 Bob Whitfield
P 96 Stafford Cliff

Stafford Cliff's photograph of Mary McCarthy's stencilled floor from *English Style* by Ken Kirkwood

With special thanks to Ron Pickless, Charles Parsons, and Paul Cheshire for their help and enthusiasm